The Road
to Recovery

Navigating Your Successful Personal Injury Case in Ontario

RICHARD AUGER and
BRENDA HOLLINGSWORTH

The
Road
to
Recovery

●● PAGE TWO

As you read through this book, please keep in mind that none of the information within should be considered legal advice. For in-depth legal information pertaining to your specific case, there is no substitute for actually consulting with an experienced personal injury lawyer who practices in Ontario.

Cataloguing in publication information is available from Library and Archives Canada.
ISBN 978-1-77458-235-0 (paperback)
ISBN 978-1-77458-236-7 (ebook)

Page Two
pagetwo.com

Edited by Scott Steedman
Copyedited by Crissy Calhoun
Cover design by Cameron McKague
Interior design by Fiona Lee

ahinjurylaw.com

To Zachary and Jordan,
the bright lights in our lives.

Contents

Introduction

For too long, the process of resolving a personal injury claim after a serious accident has been a deep, dark secret. It's only become even more perplexing in recent years, as increased lawyer advertising has moved into Ontario and started promoting the instant gratification of fast settlements.

If you're an accident victim, you will understand what we mean.

Confusion reigns for many reasons. Every jurisdiction in the world has a different legal regime that determines who you can sue and under what circumstances. The insurance industry in Ontario, with its excessively complicated car insurance system, doesn't help matters. It is the most complex insurance system for motor vehicle accidents in all of North America. Trying to figure out where to turn in the aftermath of an accident is likely to add to your pain and suffering—not bring you comfort.

Google leads you to endless stories of people who have received bags of money, while others receive nothing. Even though the bulk of online information about personal injury claims is based on American law, it's hard not to compare your own case to those on the internet. And then there are those bus ads from lawyers with big toothy smiles and great hair. At least they say they are lawyers . . .

All the noise about what you should do after an accident to protect your rights makes *our* heads hurt—and we're not the injured ones trying to recover from a serious accident.

This is why we wrote this book. Almost two decades ago, Auger Hollingsworth set out to be "a different kind" of personal injury firm. Part of our vision is to provide education to our clients. In September 2007, we published the first edition of the *Injured Victim's Guide to Fair Compensation*. We knew that there was a significant need for information about the personal injury process designed specifically for residents of Ontario, and we were right. We have since filled thousands of orders for the book. We've also published several more booklets and packed our website full of resources, guides, and tools for those considering or going through the litigation process.

The Road to Recovery combines many of these resources, and more, to give you a behind-the-curtain look at all aspects of personal injury law that matter to you as the injured person, as well as your family and loved ones, caregivers, lawyers, and professionals from different areas of practice who are there to support you. We've done our best to strip out as much legalese as possible and write in the clearest terms in order to take you through what to expect every step of the way. We've also tried to make the reading somewhat enjoyable—something not always true about the personal injury process itself!

From our experience, we know there are barriers to this process, starting with that first call to a lawyer. We've also seen what clients go through daily as they struggle in the aftermath of an accident that changed their lives.

Personal injury clients are not "corporate clients"—you come from all walks of life. Because we both started our careers as Bay Street lawyers, we know how intimidating the stages of litigation can be, and how insurance adjusters are trained to protect the interests of the insurance company. Richard's childhood—growing up in a family struggling with illness and financial hardship—provides him with particular insight into what it's like to face unpaid bills and an uncertain future.

We get it. It's impossible to know what you don't know. That's why this book is grounded in reality. We even sympathize with those of you who don't want to sue—believing that it is not a nice thing to do.

You can't change the accident or what has happened since. But knowing what to expect and why certain steps of the process happen the way they do can help you reduce uncertainty and, more important, build confidence. We're only a phone call away. While you're thinking of calling, or if you've already started the process, we hope this book becomes your guide on the road to recovery.

BRENDA AND RICHARD

1

Do I Really Have to Make That Call?

YOUR LIFE has come to a grinding halt. It's been weeks, or months, since you were seriously injured in an accident and, in a blink of an eye, your entire world turned inside out.

It's not just the physical pain that keeps you up at night, although the throbbing headaches and soreness are relentless. There's no way you'll be able to return to work. The bills are piling up, your usually tidy house is a mess, and most days you barely recognize yourself in the mirror. Your kids are needy—they are kids after all. The responsibilities for running a household, picking up groceries, even taking your kid to soccer practice are now on your spouse's shoulders. But your family can barely cope with the mounting knowledge that life has been permanently changed. None of you know what to do except get through the next day, and the next . . .

The aftermath of an accident is more than any one person, or their family, should ever have to face. The trouble is: the suffering and frustration doesn't stop with your physical or psychological injuries. There's been at least one phone call from an aggressive insurance adjuster; other people involved in the accident are also calling. If the accident was a slip and fall, it may be a nervous store owner asking for a written statement— even though you thought you gave one.

Next, add on that "great" advice you're getting from well-meaning friends and relatives. They aren't experts, but that doesn't stop them from giving you all kinds of ideas every time the topic of the accident is raised.

"You should sue." "You shouldn't sue."

"You should just put this behind you." "You should talk to the press."

"You should hire a lawyer." "Beware of lawyers; even a phone call costs money."

"Get an accountant involved." "Try a paralegal." "Talk with my therapist." "My nephew's studying law and can give you free advice." "Have you checked out Google?"

Your head hurts even more just thinking about it. You didn't ask to be injured; what happened wasn't your fault. But on top of having to learn how to walk again or cope with pain, you've been pushed into a process that involves reports and forms and statements that no one—especially those giving you their opinions right now—can begin to understand.

Press pause

....

We hear you. In fact, every day we see what people and their families go through when they've been injured in a serious accident, facing months of rehabilitation and often a lifetime coping with the consequences. We've sat at the bedside of a young person who will never walk again; we've listened to a spouse tearfully tell the story of his wife's tragic fall; and we've heard over and over again from clients how overwhelming it is to be badly hurt and not know how you are going to pay next month's rent.

What we can tell you is that there are ways to get your life back—whether you're the one who's been badly hurt, or you're close to someone in a rehabilitation facility or hospital undergoing treatment. But the process starts with something most people don't want to think about, let alone talk about—calling a lawyer. Ugh!

Take a deep breath. We are here to make things simple for you.

The elephant in the room

The idea of calling a lawyer has not been on your mind, or if it has, you've shoved the idea aside. It's the one thing we hear most in our practice. And if you're lucky, it may be that you don't need a lawyer. But before you make that decision, let's look at what's making you reluctant to call.

No doubt, you've seen advertisements for legal services. You may even feel bombarded by billboards and TV ads, depending on where you live in Ontario. Lawyers may all seem the same to you. And you are fairly certain that if you end up in their office, you won't get out without signing a contract that commits you to a strategy you don't understand and gives them the movie rights to your trial.

Next, there are the lawyer characters on television and in movies, racing about with no time to spare, always pushing to take someone to court and make them pay. Unless they are environmental lawyers, the typical TV lawyer comes across as pretty slick and self-serving. We've watched *Better Call Saul.* It doesn't paint us in a great light. You can't imagine a lawyer would have time for you. With this kind of public image, no wonder our clients often tell us how anxious they were at our first meeting!

Then there are cultural reasons. Canadians are, well, "nice," and nice people don't do things like call lawyers. It's something Americans do, of course, but we're not like *them.* On top of that, many of us value forgiveness and saying you're sorry. Suing just doesn't sound like "turning the other cheek."

Finally, there's peer pressure. Even if you figure you *should* call a lawyer, people around you start in with their advice. Is this something you really want to deal with now? Is it going to be worth it if you weren't hurt "that much"? Someone you respect, perhaps your doctor, may try to talk you out of it, or worse, the person who caused the accident—who is also a family member—says to you, "How could you do this to me?" Ouch.

It's not rocket science

Apart from those barriers, there's another reason you may be hesitating. Calling a lawyer means entering a world that you don't know or understand. At a time when you are dealing with everything from PTSD, anxiety, depression, anguish, and fearfulness to issues with sleep and concentration, you certainly don't need more complexity or questions in your life.

Take a deep breath. We are here to make things simple for you. Removing the mystery around what goes on in a law office by explaining what to expect goes a long way in making the whole process less ominous. Believe it or not, we are actual human beings doing our jobs and not slick hotshots like on TV.

For example, let's assume you were given the name of our law firm. When you call our office, you'll talk with an experienced new-client intake member of our team. They'll ask some general questions about the accident: the date, location, and a short explanation of what happened. The date is important because if there are time limits for taking certain steps (called "giving notice"), we may be able to help avoid missing a deadline that actually matters. They'll also write down your injuries, medical care received to date, and work missed.

Assuming that we think we can help, the next step is a consultation with a lawyer. What to expect at that meeting and how to prepare for it is dealt with in Chapter 3. But let's continue our sneak preview. The first meeting is held at our office, or at a rehab facility or the hospital; sometimes, it's on the phone or a virtual meeting. During the pandemic, we have met with and signed most new clients over Zoom. It has worked well, saving the injured person unnecessary travel and discomfort. Just think of it as a conversation where we ask about the accident and what caused it. We'll want to find out about your injuries; the kind of medical attention you received, either at the scene or afterwards at the hospital; your treatments; and medical coverage.

You'll have questions for us as well. Don't hold back. There's no judgment. You may not know your rights or what kind of compensation you deserve. That's for us to figure out. And we will give you our honest opinion.

Hopefully by the end of that consultation, you'll see that we're not as scary as you may have feared—no five-syllable legal terms.

It's no big deal to call a lawyer! A phone call or a consultation is just a chance to talk.

It's just not that big of a deal

Still hesitating?

It's no big deal to call a lawyer! A phone call or a consultation is just a chance to talk. It's the first step in demystifying the process. In fact, you can call a lawyer, learn more about the process, leave the office, and decide six months later whether you want to hire the lawyer (as long as time limits permit).

Often during an initial meeting with a potential client, we will notice forms were missed and we'll fill them out and send them in for you on the spot, no charge or obligation. Or we might know of a specialist or rehabilitation company that offers treatment you might not have known was available. We will warn you about the timelines that apply to your case. Why wouldn't you want that info in your back pocket, for free and with no pressure? It just makes sense.

As personal injury lawyers, we want you to feel confident that we have the experience and understanding that comes from working with hundreds of accident victims. Calling a law firm like ours is the right step to take. For those who may be advising someone they care about, such as a friend, a family member, or a professional making a referral, it is the honourable thing to do.

Whoever said "a journey of a thousand miles begins with a single step" was right.

A serious injury affects the entire family

We can't claim to have experienced what you are going through but we certainly know what it's like to care for loved ones and fear for the future. We get it, because we have a family too.

Richard's own mother was severely disabled. We can well imagine what life would have been like if her disability insurance had cut her off. We both nervously applauded when our teenaged sons got their driver's licences, knowing they would be out on Ontario's highways with all those unsafe drivers. We worry every day about our sons on the road.

Our values are why we got into this business in the first place and vowed to set up a firm that does things differently. We start by making sure that you and your family don't feel like your case is one more thing you've lost control of.

With an experienced personal injury lawyer as your guide and advisor, you know that you'll be moving in a clear, informed, and more positive direction. We'll make sure you understand what's going on and you'll have a team with you every step of the way to remove the burden as much as possible. You'll be freed up to focus your energy on your recovery, your rehabilitation, and whatever else it takes to get your life back.

Ready to look behind the curtain and find out what it would be like to work with a personal injury lawyer? The first step is choosing the right lawyer (because there's a difference—just saying).

CASE STUDY: It starts with a phone call...

Vik didn't want to go to the hospital after his car was struck from behind by a delivery truck. In fact, he told the ambulance to "go away" and instead called his wife, Anika, to pick him up. But the following day, Vik didn't feel well. Anika took him to an urgent care clinic where he was diagnosed by a medical doctor with a concussion, post-traumatic headache, and whiplash.

Vik followed his doctor's advice and rested for two weeks, but his condition didn't improve. He was in constant pain and had headaches that lasted over a week. Going back to work was out of the question, which made him even more anxious and frustrated. All of the family responsibilities now fell on Anika's shoulders.

As those pressures increased, Anika contacted Auger Hollingsworth by phone to ask what she should do. Encouraged by our conversation, she was able to get Vik to meet with us for a complimentary consultation. We went to their home to talk. Afterwards, the couple hired our firm.

Within a week, our lawyers had contacted Vik's insurance company to ensure that funding for his recommended treatment was set up through the accident benefits. We also coordinated all the necessary arrangements to get him expert medical attention.

Eventually, we were able to win Vik a seven-figure amount. It all started with his wife's phone call for help.

2

The Lawyers: Who Will Get You the Best Result?

S O, YOU'RE going to call a lawyer. Now for the big question—who to choose? You are not sure who to call. Should you call the guys on the side of the bus? Those bus ads must be expensive, you figure. They must be successful. They have a catchy phone number. That's clever. What can it hurt? Lawyers are all the same, aren't they?

We're here to tell you—we are not all the same.

But don't just take our word for it. You need to feel confident that you have the information to make the right choice. As we talked about in the last chapter, having some inside knowledge can help.

Beware of personal injury brokers

The difference between one lawyer and another isn't always obvious. The first step is to learn how different firms approach your case.

You might assume when you hire a lawyer from a personal injury law firm that you will be dealing with a full-time lawyer who works at that firm and is committed to building your case through all the necessary steps to get you the best result. Sounds like a given. It's not.

These days, there are personal injury brokers that use a lot of advertising to get as many clients as possible, and then they settle claims quickly but at a lower value. Although these brokers may keep some clients internally, many cases are farmed out to affiliate firms, junior lawyers, even paralegals or law clerks, in return for referral fees. This means that the people you are meeting are not the lawyers you are getting. The people working your case may not even be full-time, actual lawyers.

Known in the industry as "personal injury brokers" (not a very complimentary term), these companies are really, really good at advertising and signing up clients. But they don't always practice law. They refer your file out for a fee and reap the benefit of a quick settlement and move on to the next case. In short, their speciality is signing up clients, not prosecuting claims.

The reputation of the firm matters

There's another part to this story. When the insurance company and the lawyer for the defence receive the paperwork on your claim, they look up the lawyer (and firm) you have chosen. Surprise, surprise: the defence knows which lawyers and firms are going to build a case—that is, do the research, take it to discovery, take it to mediation, and, if the evidence supports the case, hold out for a higher amount and take it to trial.

The thinking goes something like this: "Firm A is always pushing to settle quickly. Let's give them a low-ball number, because we know they'll never go to trial. Firm B has a reputation for putting in the effort to get a higher value settlement. Darn. We'd better abandon the idea of a quick and low pay-off and get to work on a serious offer."

Yes, there can be a big difference...
and it's heartbreaking
....

In our practice, we see the difference between types of firms, and the result can be heartbreaking. In one case, a multiple car pile-up left two victims in need of compensation for severe injuries. We were able to negotiate a one-million-dollar settlement for our client, whereas the other victim—represented by someone with less experience—ended up with $50,000.

Sometimes we've had the opportunity to turn things around. In one instance we met with a new client who had been told by another lawyer that his case didn't meet the threshold for a car accident in Ontario. Fortunately he came to us for a second opinion. After carefully building his case, we were able to get him a six-figure compensation.

Okay, so you're going to do more than choose your firm off the side of a bus. Here are a few more tips to keep in mind.

Lawyers are not interchangeable
....

Different lawyers are trained and experienced in specific areas of the law. You don't want a real estate lawyer who dabbles in personal injury or a commercial litigator who does a few car crashes or slip and falls on the side. Think of the medical profession for a moment. If you break your leg, an ear, nose, and throat specialist isn't going to be much help. The same applies in the legal profession. Need further convincing? We are both lawyers, but we hire lawyers when we require advice outside of personal injury. For instance, to make our wills, we hired an estate lawyer, and when we need advice on employment law for our firm, we hire employment lawyers.

They say they're the best; they've even won awards

We'd love to tell you that we are the best, or even that we are experts… but we can't. It's not because we're modest. There are some statements lawyers are not permitted to make about themselves. We can tell you that we are personal injury lawyers, but that's it. We can't say that we are specialists. And as for those awards, such as "Voted World's Best" or "Award Winning"? Nope. Comparative statements like those aren't allowed either—by law.

Law firms that use this kind of advertising have been prosecuted by the Law Society of Ontario, but you'll still see these claims in promotional materials. Think of them like the late-night TV ads for exercise equipment that "melts fat away." It's hype.

You like the idea of a lower contingency rate

While most personal injury law firms do not charge upfront legal fees (you've likely heard this already), there is something called a "contingency percentage" or a "contingency rate" to know about. It's the typical arrangement for how we get paid as your lawyer. We receive a percentage of the amount we recover for you—and only after we recover the money. So, if we do not recover any money for you, we don't get paid. (The exact way this is all figured out is described in Chapter 3.)

Some lawyers promote the fact that their contingency rate is only a low percent. It sounds attractive, but if your settlement is significantly lower than you could get from a firm willing to put in the work to get a much higher settlement, that percentage won't leave you with more money in your pocket—quite likely the opposite.

It *is* possible to have a great lawyer working for you. **Don't settle for less.**

Be wary of the "quick settlement" promise

Be cautious about personal injury marketing branded with "quick settlement" promises. A low percentage sounds good, but it could be another sign that they are interested in settling fast (and low). From years of experience, we can tell you that reaching a settlement in the six figures or higher takes a lot of time (and therefore a higher contingency fee), but the end result for the client is well worth the effort.

Let's do the math. Lawyer A pushes through for a settlement but charges less for the time involved. Lawyer B builds a case and gets the higher settlement. Which would you prefer?

20% in legal fees on a $50,000 settlement = $40,000 for you

30% in legal fees on a $1,000,000 settlement = $700,000 for you

The whole issue of contingencies and contracts has just been reviewed by the Law Society of Ontario. Since July 1, 2021, changes have been made to Ontario's contingency fee regime. All contingency fee contracts are now virtually the same, with the contingency percentage as one of the only variables. Keep in mind that just because the contract is the same, it doesn't mean the lawyers are the same or the service is the same.

Holding out for a pit bull

It's commonly assumed that it's good to have an aggressive lawyer. You know the type—a lawyer who can terrorize the other side into submission with a demeanour that's constantly on a war footing, barking out scary ultimatums. This is *not* what you want, particularly in personal injury law where the emphasis is more on finesse than ferocity.

No lawyer in this field has ever been able to terrorize an insurance company, but a great personal injury lawyer can outsmart and outplay the other side. (And that is who you want!)

Will your lawyer pass the test?

The bottom line: you are looking for a firm that will be focused on putting time, effort, and money into your case to get you the best result.

Now that you know what to look for, here are few questions you can ask potential law firms to help you find the right lawyer.

How many cases do the personal injury lawyers at your firm handle at a time?

This question helps you tell if the firm is just pushing through cases (as described earlier) or actually taking the time to build each case. What if your lawyer is juggling 200 cases at a time? At our firm, the average is about 75 per lawyer. It's a complex process to get you the best result, so a lower number of cases indicates the lawyer uses an approach that's in your best interest, not theirs.

Can you explain the various steps involved in my case?

The lawyer you meet with should be able to describe the steps the firm will take to build your case. There is more to a personal injury case than gathering medical records. The firm's explanation of the various steps can provide you with assurance that the goal isn't to get a quick low-ball settlement and move on to the next case. It also gives you some idea as to

If there's one mantra you need to write down, it is this: **your lawyer is a regular person.**

the various resources the firm has available, such as medical experts, occupational therapists, physiotherapists, psychiatrists, etc.

Does your firm ever take cases to trial?

Although going to trial isn't always an indication that the personal injury lawyer firm is good at what they do, it is a good sign that they are willing and able to go to trial if the evidence supports a trial, and that's what you want.

Can I really ask these questions?

YES! If there's one mantra you need to write down, it is this: your lawyer is a regular person. Your lawyer is an advisor and consultant. You, on the other hand, are the client. This means you ask questions, you insist on information and clarification, and you follow up.

Here is another tip from the "secret lives of lawyers": we *love* questions. It's pretty much built into our DNA. It's how our system works and how we make a living. We understand questions and we expect them to be asked and answered. You need to do the same.

Red flag

If you're interviewing a law firm and your question is met with "Oh, don't worry about that," or "You don't need to ask that," consider that a red flag. You have the right to ask as many questions as you want. Start asking questions on day one to determine who to hire.

Is it the right law firm for *me*?

Finally, there is a question of fit. You are entering into a long-term relationship. A good fit means you feel confident about working together. Sure, you are looking for experience and reputation, but you also want your lawyer to be a good person, someone who is compassionate and sincere.

Do you have to like the law firm? Think of it this way. Your law firm is going to advocate on your behalf, which means talking and negotiating with others to get the best result. They are more likely to succeed if they are likable.

You don't have to be your lawyer's BFF, but they should give you reason to respect them. This goes for everything: from how they treat you and listen to you, to whether or not their jacket is clean, to if they remembered to shave. Don't overlook anything that makes you uneasy because you think it doesn't matter "law"-wise. You shouldn't ever work with a lawyer when you suspect they've given you a lot of BS, or they're making you feel less than, not worthy, difficult, or unheard.

It *is* possible to have a great lawyer working for you. Don't settle for less.

3

The First Meeting: Come as You Are and Give It to Us Straight

YOUR FIRST meeting with the lawyer is coming right up. Uneasy? Excited? Ready? Still not sure you should be talking with us?

Take a deep breath. You are worth it. It's worth the investment of your time to find out what your options are by talking with a lawyer. There's nothing you have to do ahead of time, but it's worth going through a few expectations and busting some myths.

Come as you are: no prep, no judgment, no homework

Your first meeting with a law firm (the "free consultation") is risk-free and judgment free. During the course of the meeting, you'll get a good sense of whether or not this is a law firm you want to hire. Like that first telephone call, the consultation is not a big deal—it's just a meeting.

Following the initial intake phone call, we meet you wherever is convenient for you: at our office, a rehab facility, the hospital, or virtually. Expect the meeting to last anywhere between 45 minutes and two hours.

We'll ask questions about the accident, your injuries, treatment, and insurance, so information and documents related to these topics is helpful. If you don't have time or energy to look, or aren't sure what you have, we can sort all that out later and let you know. Right now, we're more interested in meeting you and hearing your story, not checking off a list of "homework" to see what you've brought us.

There's no right way to show up. Just come.

Over the years, we've found that no two people approach this meeting in the same way or with the same expectations. If the meeting is in person, some arrive with a binder full of information, organized by tab dividers; others hand us a plastic bag full of wrinkled documents. Many don't bring much or anything at all. All of this is fine. More and more, information comes later via email.

What are we going to ask about?

The best way to prepare for this meeting is to think of it as a conversation.

We'll ask about the accident scene and how the accident happened. If photographs were taken at the scene, these are very helpful, particularly if there is any debate later as to what someone thinks they remember. If the accident was a car collision and the police were called, there will be an official Motor Vehicle Accident Report, sometimes with witness names. This is one of many reports we'll be looking at on your behalf. There's a chance that the police were called and didn't come. This means we'll use what was recorded at the collision centre and the notes we take to reconstruct the scene. If the accident was a slip and fall, we'll want to know about the weather conditions that day, what you had on your feet, and if anyone took a photo of the scene.

We'll also ask questions about your injuries, including your psychological state, medical treatment, rehab, etc. What kind of medical attention did you receive, either at the scene or afterwards at the hospital? Perhaps you didn't realize how badly you were hurt until the next day? A doctor's record will confirm your condition, and we'll be able to use that report to build your case. Not everyone goes to the hospital. In fact, we've seen many instances where an accident victim refused to even get in an ambulance. What's important is that you did seek out medical attention. We'll get the details on that from you.

The conversation may feel difficult when we ask about how your injury has impacted your life. Are you able to work? Can you manage daily tasks, like buying groceries, walking your kid to school, or taking a shower?

Finally, we'll want to know about your insurance coverage, whether or not you've applied for benefits, and anything else you want to unload about insurance! At that time, we'll explain things like how insurance companies and injury claims work, so you begin to feel a little more knowledgeable about what is, without doubt, a mind-bending, complex process.

Oops, what if I say the wrong thing?

Some people worry that they haven't got their facts quite right, or they may have missed something. Of course, it's helpful if you can provide a clear, accurate account, with addresses and witness names. You're not on trial during the meeting. We are

We are committed to helping you get the money you deserve—**and to make sure justice is served.**

all human and no human has a perfect memory. Our role is to review all the details over the days and weeks ahead as they appear in the various reports and records, and we make sure nothing gets missed. If something needs correcting, adjusting, clarifying, even fixing, we manage it on your behalf.

There is nothing that you could say to us that is wrong in our meeting (unless you don't tell the truth). No one gets a gold star for answering questions a certain way. There is no judgment.

The good, the bad, and the ugly: we want to hear it all

Okay, so *maybe* there's something you really don't want to tell us. Like you had a large taco salad in your lap while you were driving, or your favourite song was blaring over your headphone when you slipped on a broken piece of pavement. We need to know it all, and there's no risk or judgment in telling us.

This is thanks to "solicitor-client privilege." Whatever you tell a lawyer in a meeting (even before you hire that lawyer) is confidential and protected. It means you can be totally honest with us and know that we're not going to use it against you or your case. And it means that we know we don't have to worry there might be surprises along the way because we didn't have all the information. Here's an example:

> You're stopped in your car at a red light and are hit from behind. You did nothing wrong and the fault is entirely with the other driver. But you did check your cell phone while you were waiting for the light to change. This detail is not going to impact your case: it's not particularly "ugly" and only a bit "bad," but it is something we need to know so we're not caught by surprise later on.

What if you don't want my case?

The worst that can happen at this first meeting would be to find out that you do not have a case that we can handle for you. If this is true, it's better to find out now, not months or years down the road.

There are a few reasons why this may be the outcome:

- If you had a car accident, it could be that we think your case doesn't meet the verbal threshold in Ontario for suing for "pain and suffering." This is part of a legal threshold requirement that can be a complex legal and factual determination. In simple terms, if your car accident did not result in you having injuries that are serious and permanent, you will not win a claim even if you were actually hurt and not at fault. Is that fair? Absolutely not. The *Ontario Insurance Act* is incredibly unfair to many accident victims. The point of this law is to eliminate the right to sue for injuries that are not considered serious enough to go to court.

- Let's say the other party was negligent and you were almost hurt as a result. You may be worried about what the person may do to others in the future. It can be difficult for an individual and their family to separate bad behaviour from serious damage. Unfortunately, a case cannot be built around behaviour that *almost* caused an injury—even if it's clear that the other person involved was a careless jerk.

- Another common reason for turning down a case has to do with time. Most Ontario personal injury claims where the injured person is an adult must be started within two years of the date of the accident. If your case is too close to the limitation period, we may feel that there just isn't enough time to gather all the records and documents and properly build a case.

- Sometimes we determine that a case is doomed because we won't be able to establish negligence on the part of someone else. For example, if you fall on the sidewalk but there was nothing wrong with the sidewalk, you probably don't have a case, even if you were badly injured. (However, when in doubt, it's always best to get a lawyer's perspective in a case like this. We may detect a problem with the sidewalk that you didn't recognize.)

- Finally, we may feel that we are not the best team to handle your case for another reason. For example, your situation might be outside our area of expertise. If that happens, whenever possible, we will direct you to a lawyer or firm we know and trust.

Some of this may be upsetting, yes. But turning down a case is a sign of a good lawyer (remember the lawyers who advertise on buses?). The last thing you want is for someone to take on your case without a proper analysis of its chance of success. This just wastes your time and emotional energy.

Maybe you are reading this list thinking, "Uh oh. That's going to be me." Come to the consultation anyway. Don't fall into the trap of doing your own "legal analysis." People who are not trained lawyers are often not great at assessing fault or figuring out if a case meets the threshold. Why not hear it from the horse's mouth instead of making an assumption?

Who else can come to the meeting?

You may want to have a friend or family member come with you for moral support. Maybe your best friend is absolutely insistent she come. This can get a little tricky.

Remember "the bad and the ugly" discussion earlier in this chapter? A friend or family member could make you reluctant to tell us certain details, which isn't good for either of us. If they are also a witness to the accident or even to the impact of your injuries on your life, we can't have you in the conversation together. For these reasons, we may ask them to wait in a separate room. But as long as we know ahead of time, we can make them feel welcome and manage the situation for you—without any awkward pauses or apologies!

Need an interpreter? Just let us know what you need in advance.

There also are times when someone has suffered a severe injury, such as a brain injury, and a power of attorney is named. This individual attends the meeting with you because they are now the one making decisions on your behalf. Those decisions include choosing a lawyer, signing the contract, and following through on your lawsuit.

If you are in a trauma centre, a team that includes a psychologist, psychiatrist, and social worker will give an opinion on whether you can name a power of attorney. In our experience, there are only a few cases where this is *not* possible. Otherwise, a guardian can be appointed (for adults who lack capacity or for an injured child).

Signing on the dotted line

We're lawyers, so you know there are going to be papers to sign. Assuming that we agree to work together, the final step is a contract called the Contingency Fee Agreement. Sometimes lawyers call it a retainer agreement, although you don't actually have to pay a retainer.

The Contingency Fee Agreement is the contract that spells out what you are hiring the lawyer to do for you and other details about the relationship and the terms—in particular,

A good lawyer makes sure you have time to read the agreement before you sign it, and they will walk you through each section, paraphrasing the content to explain what it means.

who pays for what and how. For instance, on top of legal services (the fee for our work), there are out-of-pocket expenses ("disbursements") that have to be paid to advance your case over the coming months: everything from ordering medical records to covering courier fees.

A good lawyer makes sure you have time to read the agreement before you sign it, and they will walk you through each section, paraphrasing the content to explain what it means. Think of the Contingency Fee Agreement as our protection for you so you know what the lawyer will do, how much you will be charged, etc.

Here are the main parts of the agreement:

- Confirm that there are no upfront fees or deposits

- Confirm that the lawyer is paid a percentage of the settlement or judgment, and if there is no compensation awarded to you, the lawyer doesn't take a fee

- Specify that percentage amount

- Explain how disbursements (the firm's out-of-pocket expenses) are paid

- Deal with issues such as cancelling a contract, and what happens if the case doesn't settle

The bottom line? Since July 1, 2021, the Contingency Fee Agreement in Ontario has been standardized for all lawyers. However, make sure you understand what it means, particularly the money part. The way our firm has structured the agreement, you can avoid ever being out of pocket if your case results in a settlement.

Once the agreement is signed, you'll also be asked to sign authorizations for us to start gathering evidence, such as medical records, the ambulance report, the 911 recording, and so on. This is a much simpler document—promise.

How we get paid

The expenses we incur while building your case are called disbursements (out-of-pocket expenses such as paying for experts, ordering reports, etc.). When we receive the final settlement amount, we deduct these disbursements from it first. Then we subtract our fee, as described in the signed contingency agreement. There also could be other parties to pay, such as the Ontario Health Insurance Plan (OHIP) or a long-term disability carrier. If we accept a settlement on your behalf, you will know how much goes into your pocket before the deal is finalized.

We usually ask the defence for a contribution to legal fees as part of the settlement (if there is no trial). The contribution to legal fees is called "costs." Costs are typically 15 percent of the first $100,000, 10 percent of everything after that, plus HST. Where possible, we push for this to be paid by the defence on top of the settlement amount, which means some of the contingency percentage you pay is covered. Most of the time, however, the settlement is negotiated as a lump sum with the costs portion rolled into the overall settlement.

We are committed to helping you get all of the money you deserve—and to make sure justice is served.

Why we talk about cost insurance when you hire us

If you lose your case, you could be out of pocket for paying disbursements and legal fees for the other side. (You would never have to pay our legal fees.) Cost insurance, also known as "after the event" (ATE) insurance, covers your exposure to defence costs in this situation. It also covers our firm's disbursements if you have to walk away from the case. We'll advise you on whether you should consider buying cost insurance and how much you should buy. Most people do buy it because it provides that extra level of comfort, although it is very rare to need it. The neat thing about cost insurance is that if you do walk away or if the case is not successful, you don't pay any insurance premium.

This all sounds great,
but are you going to win my case?

At our firm, we get favourable results for our clients. We'd like to say it's because we are brilliant, but to be fair, we are successful partly because we take on cases that we believe will have a positive result. Success for us is not *if* you get a settlement, but how much you receive. We have achieved over 100 million dollars for our clients. We hope to add your settlement to our growing tally.

Very occasionally, we will recommend that a client abandon a case before it goes too far—and for good reason. Perhaps the injuries turn out not to be permanent or as severe as feared, and the person recovers (good news). Or maybe once we have all the information, the facts don't support a finding of negligence against the other side. These sorts of cases are rare, but they do happen.

Whew! Did that, got the T-shirt

No two people approach their first lawyer meeting the same way or with the same expectations. As personal injury lawyers, however, we can tell you that almost everyone leaves that first meeting with a shift in their mindset.

There are definite reasons for feeling relieved. If your accident was a motor vehicle collision, hopefully a light went on for you. We mentioned how the auto insurance regime in Ontario is known to be the *most* complicated in North America. The first meeting makes all of your anxiety about this go away; a weight is lifted off your shoulders when you realize that someone knows how it works and will put that skill and knowledge to work for you.

In addition, all the other anxiety you had about talking to a lawyer or figuring out what to do next (including filling out all those insurance forms) lessens. You have handed over the stress, the uncertainty, and the complexity to us so we can manage everything for you.

If we could see the thought bubble over your head as we wrap up that first meeting, it would say, "Whew. We're going to get through this."

CASE STUDY: Managing the bad and the ugly

Roni suffered catastrophic injuries when he was a passenger in a car that slammed into a cement wall and burst into flames. There were several details that complicated the case. Roni had been drinking at a bar with a friend and his friend was intoxicated when he got behind the wheel (he was later convicted of impaired driving causing bodily harm and served time in jail as a result). It also turned out that the driver only had his G2 licence, which meant he was not permitted to drive with any amount of alcohol in his system. The insurance company argued that it did not have to cover him because he had violated the insurance policy. As for Roni, he did not have his own car insurance to cover him.

This is a case that had a lot of "bad and ugly"—but drawing on our firm's criminal defence experience, we were able to conduct a very thorough examination of the tavern that served the booze and identify weaknesses in its policies and practices relating to the service of alcohol. We sued the bar that overserved Roni and the driver without any regard to how they would get home safely. We also located an insurance policy that covered the owner of the vehicle despite the drinking.

Ultimately, we achieved a seven-figure settlement in addition to a lump sum for long-term disability for Roni that provided him with the security he and his family needed.

4

Insurance:
Someone
Has to Pay

WHEN YOU'VE been seriously injured in an accident, the bills start piling up. There are all of the out-of-pocket expenses related to your injury. Sometimes, you can't return to work, and you're not sure if you are ever going to be able to do so. There are lots of services for hire that could make life easier, such as housekeeping, child care, and specialized therapies, as well as products like assistive devices to help with your recovery. But all of these things cost money.

Someone has to pay.

This is where insurance comes in—your own insurance and the insurance purchased by the person at fault who caused the accident.

Once you've hired a personal injury lawyer, you no longer have to deal with the insurance company or the adjuster (hurray!). But you do have to help us when we ask for various documents and records. This chapter explains how the system works, what we do on your behalf, and why.

Insurance and motor vehicle accidents

Let's first look at insurance as it relates to motor vehicle accidents, and then insurance for other kinds of accidents, such as slip and falls. If your accident didn't involve a motor vehicle, you can skip this complicated part of the chapter and go straight to page 63. Otherwise, brace yourself to learn about the complex world of motor vehicle insurance in Ontario. It's not an easy read, so we suggest you use this chapter as a reference rather than try to absorb it all at once! By the way, when we say motor vehicles, we mean cars, trucks, motorcycles, buses (sometimes), and even snowmobiles.

Statutory accident benefits in Ontario

When there is a motor vehicle accident, there are two different claims available to injured persons or their loved ones: statutory accident benefits, which are commonly known as "no fault benefits," and liability claims, which are the claims for compensation from the person who caused the injuries. Just to make things more complicated, these are also known as bodily injury claims.

Almost everyone involved in a motor vehicle accident in Ontario is entitled to statutory accident benefits, *regardless of who caused the accident.* In most cases, these benefits are paid by your own insurance policy, even if your own car was parked in your driveway when the accident happened. If you don't have car insurance, and no one in your home has car insurance, you will likely be covered by the policy of the other vehicle involved in the accident. Almost everyone is covered by a policy, including pedestrians and cyclists (with a government resource of last resort).

Accident benefits have three different levels depending on your injuries: catastrophic (CAT), non-catastrophic (non-CAT), and minor injury (MIG).

CAT applies when the individual becomes quadriplegic, paraplegic, or suffers another form of serious injury. The middle category (non-CAT) is more common. The most common types of injuries in this group are fractures and head injuries.

The rest fall in the minor injury stream, even though the injury may not feel minor. Not everyone who has suffered a minor injury needs a lawyer, but if that injury isn't healing or a psychological injury develops, it may evolve into something that falls into a higher category.

The total amount of the benefits available to you (also known as the "policy limits") varies depending on whether your injury is CAT, non-CAT, or MIG, as does the eligibility period. Figuring out your category and what benefits you are entitled to can be very difficult. The form letter sent by the insurance company doesn't help; for many people, it's incomprehensible. And to make matters more complicated, the amounts of the benefits and even the exact benefits themselves change from time to time. For example, between 2010 and 2018, accident benefit laws changed 17 times! (That right there is a reason to choose a lawyer who handles personal injury full time.)

Here's an outline of the major benefits offered through statutory accident benefits in Ontario:

- **Attendant care:** This is money available to pay someone to help you with your personal care, such as dressing, bathing, wound care, leg shaving, hair drying, administering medicine, and many other very personal types of care. To qualify for this benefit, you need to be assessed by a health care professional, most often an occupational therapist. The insurance company pays for the assessment.

- **Housekeeping:** If your injuries are CAT or you've purchased optional benefits, there's no need to tolerate the mountains of dirty laundry piling up. Currently, there is an amount available for housekeeping and home maintenance so that household tasks can be kept up while you're recuperating. Most insurers need receipts, but the work can still be done by family members. You usually, but not always, need an assessment for this too. Again, the insurance company pays for the assessment.

- **Income replacement:** If you are off the job for more than one week, this benefit will pay you 70 percent of your gross weekly earnings, up to a fixed maximum that changes from time to time. To be eligible, the test varies depending on the length of time you are off work. There is a form your employer completes for you to get this money.

- **Caregiving:** If you are the primary caregiver for children or a disabled adult and have purchased this benefit, there may be a weekly benefit available to you if you can't claim the income replacement benefit. The amount varies depending on the number of people you look after. Your need for this benefit is also assessed, usually by an occupational therapist.

- **Non-earner payment:** If you were not working and were not a caregiver, there is a weekly benefit payable to you if you're unable to live a normal life after the accident. You don't get this benefit until six months post-accident and you will be sent for an assessment before you qualify.

- **Medical and rehabilitation costs:** There is a pot of money available to fund your rehabilitation and medical expenses beyond what is covered by OHIP and which are necessary to help you get better or reintegrate into your life. The benefits available under this category range from prescriptions and physiotherapy to an accessible car and home. The amount available and the timing of when it is available vary depending on whether you are at the CAT, non-CAT, or MIG level.

- **Visitors' expenses:** Family members who visit you at the hospital or during your convalescence are entitled to be reimbursed for their mileage. There is no prescribed rate

Our help can increase your chances of **getting the benefits you deserve.**

for this mileage. The only real test to qualify for these benefits is that they be reasonable and necessary.

Applying for the benefits—not as easy as you'd think

The statutory accident benefits are not automatic. You have to apply for them, using forms provided to you by the insurance company. Some of the benefits require your doctor or other health care provider to complete a certificate that indicates you need the services. If your insurance company does not send you the forms, we can help you access them on the internet.

You don't sue to access these benefits. However, without legal advice, you may not receive all of the benefits to which you are entitled. If you are denied a benefit you should have received, a lawyer can launch a challenge for you. That's why it's a good idea to have a lawyer acting on your behalf, in your best interests. In all likelihood, you'll be in no condition mentally or physically to handle the type of stress that comes with applying for these benefits.

As your lawyers, we assist with the process, which is a great relief to anyone trying to figure it out. Our help can increase your chances of getting the benefits you deserve.

What's the end game with accident benefits?

One thing the accident benefit insurance company does not tell you at the beginning of your accident benefit claim is that at some point you may want—and they may want—to pay out your claim as a lump sum.

Beginning 12 months after the date of your accident, you may be approached by the insurance company to settle. Sometimes it's a good idea. Sometimes it's not!

If you're not a lawyer or in the insurance industry, you (understandably) have no way of knowing what settlement amount the insurer could possibly pay out. Many who settle their own accident benefits claims to do so for an amount that's less than what they need and less than what they should get under their policy.

For example, in 2008, a young man met with us before he accepted a "final offer." His accident benefit insurer had offered a payment of $14,000, and although this seemed like a lot of money to him, he decided to get a second opinion on what his case was worth. When we itemized all the types of claims he was eligible for, it was well over the $25,000 mark, and that was with a conservative view of his expected recovery.

If you are working with a lawyer during the first year after your accident, we can also help you make decisions to maximize a potential accident benefit settlement. Small decisions about treatment choices can have a big impact on a settlement offer down the road.

Dealing with your insurance company

There are many ways that your legal representation can help you deal with your insurance company. Here are just a few of the kinds of issues we've helped our clients manage:

- If the accident benefit insurance company is denying a benefit that you are entitled to, we'll fight that dispute at the Licence Appeal Tribunal.

- There may be benefits you're not aware of. We can set up an assessment for benefits such as income replacement or attendant care.

- We'll advocate for moving you into the catastrophic injury category if your injuries are very serious. We have had an excellent success rate on disputed CAT claims. We'll set up assessments for catastrophic injuries as early as possible and repeat them at various intervals, to support the claim.

- Following the first anniversary of your accident, we can help you to negotiate a lump-sum payout of part or all of your accident benefits.

- We can help maximize your accident benefits claim if you were injured in an accident and you are the at-fault driver (and therefore not entitled to any other compensation).

- If you're pursuing both an accident benefits claim and a lawsuit against the driver who caused your accident (explained below), each are on a parallel but separate track, intermingled with a complicated system of deductibles. None of it is easy to figure out or to manage. We can be sure you claim the right type of compensation from each insurer.

Tort claims

Unfortunately, we mean bodily injury, not French pastries, when we mention "torts"! If you've been injured in a motor vehicle accident, you may have a claim against the driver and owner of the vehicle that hit you. These proceedings are called "tort actions." This is true if you are a driver, passenger, pedestrian, or cyclist.

In the simplest scenario, you'll make a claim against the at-fault driver and owner of the vehicle, called a liability claim. If that person has insurance coverage (and in Ontario they are required to), their insurance company will step into their shoes and respond on their behalf.

Whether or not you have a claim depends in part on who or what caused the accident.

Whether or not you have a claim **depends in part on who or what caused the accident.**

If you and you alone caused the accident—unless your vehicle malfunctioned or there was some other external issue in play—you will not likely have a bodily injury claim against another driver. You will likely have an accident benefit claim, but that may be it. However, before deciding that you have zero chance at a liability claim, consider speaking to a lawyer about why the accident happened. Did your vehicle malfunction? It happens, although rare. Was there a road defect? Again, rare but possible. If your injuries are serious, it may be worth turning over every last stone to see if there is a possible path to compensation. We'd be happy to discuss the options with you.

To sue for pain and suffering in Ontario, you have to prove that your injuries are serious and permanent and important, or disfiguring. The legal threshold is not all that straightforward; you want legal advice about whether or not you meet it before making important decisions about your case. We've said it before: don't make assumptions about whether you meet the threshold, and don't believe the insurance company if it tells you that you don't. Get advice from your own lawyer who knows the law and has no hidden agenda to dissuade you from suing.

The other hurdle you must jump before suing for pain and suffering is the deductible. In Ontario, there is a "deductible" that comes off your damages for pain and suffering if those damages are less than a set amount. This deductible is set by the Ontario government and is indexed to inflation, so it changes every year. We'll tell you what the current deductible is when we meet and we'll tell you what it is when we are settling your case.

In addition to pain and suffering, the bodily injury claim can include your out-of-pocket expenses and loss of income, your future medical care costs, housekeeping costs, loss of pension, loss of competitive advantage, and many other types of damages (to the extent that those damages are not covered by the accident benefits). There can also be compensation for your family members who have lost your care and companionship because of the accident. (This is outlined in detail in Chapter 6, page 96.) Keep in mind that even if you don't meet the threshold to sue for pain and suffering, you can still claim your economic losses. The insurance company won't tell you that, but we will!

Dealing with an insurance company is not for the faint of heart

Accidents are often complex events and fault is not always all one-sided. The financial ramifications associated with sorting out these complexities in the case can have a massive impact on the injured victim's future. This is why it is so important to hire an experienced personal injury lawyer to investigate, determine responsibility, support you, and defend your legal right.

Don't let those days and weeks slip away before getting advice!

In Ontario, the law places very strict time restrictions and requirements on the right to pursue a claim.

Most motor vehicle accident claims on behalf of an adult must be started within two years of the date of the accident in Ontario, which is known as the "limitation period." While there are exceptions, they are few and far between. For children, the limitation period starts to run on their 18th birthday, which means most cases expire on the day before their 20th birthday. Keep in mind that the case has to be filed with the court before the limitation period expires; a letter is not enough.

Apart from the limitation period, there is the "notice period." In order to be paid interest on the damages, you are required to give a form of notice to the at-fault parties within 120 days of the accident.

You want to stay on the right side of the notice and limitation periods.

Why it's easier to deal with accident benefits than the at-fault driver's insurance

Statutory accident benefits are "first-party claims." When you first purchased this kind of insurance, you made a contract with your insurance company: that contract says you agree to pay premiums and they owe you "a duty of good faith" to treat you fairly. You might have to negotiate back and forth to agree on a number, but you should get an amount that is fair.

In a first-party claim, the insurance company has a contractual duty to co-operate with you and to pay you for losses

After you have a motor vehicle accident, **you have seven days to report it to your insurance company, regardless of who is at fault.**

incurred under the policy—at least, this is the intention. In reality, first-party insurers regularly try to withhold benefits from their own customers. That's why we are constantly pursuing benefits at the Licence Appeal Tribunal. Your accident benefit insurer may be friendly to you, but they are not really on your side. Don't let your guard down.

Third-party claims are a *completely* different story! Here, we're talking liability (who's at fault) and a different "pot" of insurance money. When you've been injured and it is someone else's fault, you can commence a claim against the other person who was driving and the person who owns the vehicle (or against the corporation that owns the vehicle). You are asking for compensation for loss and damages not covered by the first-party benefits. This is where we come in as your personal injury lawyers.

You have to prove your losses *and* prove that the driver was negligent before there will be a payout.

The at-fault party's insurance provider typically steps in and defends them and/or indemnifies them (which means the at-fault party's insurance company would pay the settlement or judgment). In a third-party claim, the insurance company has no duty to you; instead, it has a duty to its insured to protect them from you!

Reporting the accident: beware of those early "insurance" conversations

After you have a motor vehicle accident, you have seven days to report it to your insurance company, regardless of who is at fault. When you call, you will give your insurer basic facts, such as the date and time of accident, a general description of what happened, and so on. You should make this call even if you were driving someone else's vehicle.

Remember the following: you must co-operate with your own insurance company by answering the questions. Your insurance company will also send you the accident benefit forms.

The other person, the at-fault party, will do the same. Their call, of course, alerts their insurance company that you are likely to make a third-party liability claim. As you can imagine, alarm bells sound (metaphorically). There is a chance that the adjuster on the other side will try to get a statement from you. Don't give one!

- You don't have to co-operate with the other person's insurance company, and you should not. Tell them that you are not prepared to make a statement. If they continue to bother you, tell them to go away.

- In some instances, by coincidence, your insurance policy is with the same company as the at-fault party. Again, be careful if you receive a call from an adjuster. Ask, "Are you calling on behalf of my policy or someone else's policy?"

The three "buckets" of auto insurance coverage in Ontario

1. Third-party liability coverage

This section of your automobile insurance policy protects you if someone else is killed or injured or their property is damaged. It will pay for claims as a result of lawsuits against you up to the limit of your coverage, and it will pay the costs of settling claims. By law, you must carry a minimum of $200,000 in third-party liability coverage but options exist to increase the minimum amount. Most people in Ontario have $1 million or $2 million in liability coverage.

When you are injured in an accident, it is the other driver's third-party liability coverage that responds to the claim.

2. First-party coverage: statutory accident benefits coverage

This section of your automobile insurance policy provides you with benefits if you are injured in an automobile accident, regardless of who caused the accident, and covers categories such as supplementary medical, rehabilitation and attendant care, caregiver, and non-earner and income replacement benefits. Options exist to increase most of these coverages.

3. First-party coverage: direct compensation–property damage (DC-PD) coverage

This section of your automobile insurance policy covers damage to your vehicle or its contents, and for loss of use of your vehicle or its contents, if another person was at fault for the accident. It is called direct compensation because even though someone else causes the damage, you collect directly from your own insurer. Most lawyers don't get involved in this part of the insurance claim.

The Ontario auto insurance regime has some great features

You're afraid that the guy who caused your accident didn't have enough—or any—insurance. Now what? It's okay. Ontario insurance law is complicated, but it has some excellent features that most people don't know about.

For example, if a driver injures you in a hit and run and can't be identified, you are protected by something called "unidentified motorist coverage." You are also covered even if the other driver has no insurance. In certain US states, like New Hampshire, vehicle insurance isn't mandatory. If this is the case, your own insurance company steps up to provide third-party liability benefits, known as "underinsured motorist coverage."

There also is a benefit called "family protection endorsement," which provides significant protection—up to the limits of your liability coverage—if the person at fault is either not insured or doesn't have enough insurance to cover what you require. You should make sure you have this coverage. Call your insurance agent to ask if you have it and, if not, add it. It is very cheap to add onto a policy, so almost everyone has it.

Your own insurance—words to the wise

By law, every driver in Ontario must carry a minimum of $200,000 in third-party liability coverage, but you can increase that amount. Most people carry $1 million; we recommend that you have at least $2 million. The difference in monthly payments is small compared to the risk if you should be at fault in an accident where someone is seriously injured. One million won't cover the settlement amount, and your home, and even your future wages, could be used to cover the shortfall.

Insurance for slip and falls
and other claims of negligence
....

If you've been able to follow this discussion on motor vehicle collision claims, you'll have no trouble following how legal claims for slip and falls and other areas of negligence work. For the most part, it's much less complicated.

Let's say you slipped on ice in front of the library or fell down steps inside a store when you went to grab a handrail that wasn't there. If you can prove that you suffered an injury of some nature and that it resulted from the negligence of someone in control of the property where you fell, usually the owner, you likely have a claim.

This is why, as step one, we determine who owns the location where you fell. Sometimes that means we do a property search. Other times, we are looking at a map or a Google satellite image to see who owns the property.

Businesses, condo corporations, property maintenance companies, retailers, governments, and so on all carry some type of insurance to cover liability (fault). Even an organization that's running an event, such as a marathon or a bike rally, takes out event liability insurance for the duration of the event.

We only pursue a claim for negligence if there is liability insurance carried by the person responsible for the negligence (unless that person is very wealthy or it is a corporation with a lot of assets). So, if you were at a friend's rental home, you may be out of luck unless the landlord was responsible for the area of the fall. Not everyone has a homeowner's insurance policy that covers liability. Even if you win the judgment, you won't be able to collect any money.

Private homes take more digging, to be sure. Mortgage companies typically require insurance, which means there will be an insurance policy if the owners are still paying a mortgage. Or if you fall at someone's home and they are renting, their landlord will likely have insurance.

Is it always insurance that pays?

Governments and large companies have a couple of pots of money to settle claims. In addition to liability insurance from an insurance company, they have what is known as "self-insurance": money allocated internally for claims each year. Sometimes it can be easier to settle claims if the amount you are seeking is within the amount of money set aside for this type of claim.

There also are instances where self-insurance will be supplemented by an insurance policy. This is the case for the 2019 Westboro bus crash in Ottawa, which killed three people and injured 23. The lawsuits collectively demanded more than $180 million from the City of Ottawa; the insurers will cover most of the amount after the city paid out the first $3 million.

There are instances where we look to more than one party for compensation. Maybe, for example, you reached for a can of cola on top of a display at your local grocery story. The next thing you know, the entire pyramid of cans fell on top of you because the display hadn't been put together properly. In this situation, we may sue both the cola company and the store. They, in turn, sort out between them who is responsible.

Fell in your own home? Sorry, you can't insure yourself for your own negligence on your own property—unless you rent and have a landlord who is responsible for the area of the fall. This is why you should speak to a lawyer.

Yes, there are deadlines

If a slip and fall occurs on municipal property, you must provide the municipality with written notice of the fall—including the time, the date, and the location—within ten days of the incident. Notice can be made by service on the City Clerk or by registered mail. This tight timeline is another good reason to get advice from a lawyer right away.

There are tight timelines that apply to slip and falls that happen due to ice and snow on private property. Speaking with a lawyer as soon as possible after your accident will ensure that you don't miss an important deadline.

Bring on the lawyers

Hopefully it's pretty obvious now why personal injury lawyers deal with their clients' insurance companies, either because of a motor vehicle accident or another kind of personal injury claim. The discussion that follows applies equally to both categories of claims.

Once hired, we immediately assume responsibility for the advancement of your case. We help you prove that another person failed to carry out a duty of care (that is, they acted negligently); that these actions, directly or indirectly, harmed the injured person (that is, they caused the accident or the loss or damage suffered); and that this person therefore bears liability.

In addition, we determine a dollar value for your losses, including pain and suffering, past and future income loss, future health care, and so on. To do so, we have to demonstrate—through evidence, expert opinion, and case law—that your case is worth that dollar value.

We do all of this to get the insurance company to pay.

Dealing with insurance adjusters

The insurance adjuster, sometimes known as a claims analyst, is the person who deals with claims. Their job is to look at your case, investigate liability (who's at fault), and come up with an assessment in order to settle your case or tell you why they will not pay anything.

They do this all the time, and the good ones have a sense of what cases are worth. Understand, however, that they almost always are going to undervalue the claim. Remember, they work for the insurance company: their goal is to close the case for the least amount possible and as soon as possible. They are typically given bonuses for closing files quickly, which gives them a reason to push for a settlement.

Never forget that all insurance companies (including your own) are in business only to increase profits. This means their main objective is to pay out as little as possible to injured people. This is why you want an experienced personal injury lawyer.

Like tax collectors and parking ticket officers, insurance adjusters have a bit of a bad rap. Hollywood will never make a movie featuring the good deeds of the justice-seeking insurance adjuster. In saying that, however, we find that the vast majority of insurance adjusters are decent professionals who are just doing their jobs. A responsible adjuster understands that your case has a value and will listen to reason when presented with the evidence and the case law that supports the dollar value.

Never forget that all insurance companies (including your own) are **in business only to increase profits.**

Savvy personal injury lawyers know what evidence the adjuster needs to get the authority to settle for the amount we want for you.

Responsible insurance adjusters will change an unreasonable position when presented with credible evidence.

Can't we all just get along?

Clients often ask us if we can work out a settlement over a friendly call on the telephone. This can happen, and if we think we can work out a fair settlement for you this way, we'll make that call.

By its nature, however, the process is adversarial. Make no mistake. There's no screaming or yelling involved (at least, not from us), but as your lawyers, we are looking at the accident from an entirely different perspective than the insurance company.

The insurance company is under instruction from its share-holders to close your claim for the minimum payout possible, and the adjusters are trained in how to say no.

The plaintiff (that's you) has to prove entitlement in order to get a settlement that covers your losses, current and future. A solution won't (usually) be found over a friendly cup of tea. We have to present evidence that shows the risk faced by the insurance company if it doesn't pay, and we have to demonstrate through preparation and reputation that we are ready to take the case to trial (through a lawsuit) in order to get the money.

Is there ever an easy way out?

If your injuries are relatively minor and your economic losses are fairly well defined, we can negotiate a settlement without litigation by dealing directly with the insurance adjuster. This is discussed in detail in Chapter 13 on settlement. However, if you're dealing with an injured child, or your own injuries have affected your livelihood, or are going to involve expenses in the future for care and rehabilitation, it can take months or even years to determine losses (medical and financial).

The same can apply to liability, particularly in complex cases. We represented a woman in her 50s who was involved in an accident with a pedestrian that included a railway crossing and a transport truck. The police force responsible for the roadway took 18 months to complete its review and assessment of the accident site. None of the insurance companies involved were going to even start a settlement discussion until this report was available. So, even though the client's injuries had stabilized much earlier, no discussion was possible until the police filed their report.

When negotiations aren't the answer

Let's assume your case is not going to be resolved at the adjuster level. The process moves to the next step, where we file a statement of claim on your behalf. Once this happens, it's no secret that the plan is to proceed with a lawsuit and, if needed, go all the way to trial. The at-fault party responds by sending the claim to their insurance company, which then hires their own lawyer. The insurance defence lawyer now represents that person (the at-fault party). In complex cases, there are multiple parties and claims, which make the legal issues even more complicated.

Again, your lawyer is going to take care of this for you. But it's going to add to the length of time the case now takes (perhaps up to two years) and the amount of work that needs to be done to sort it all out.

Suing sounds so mean

Yes, on paper, you name a person you are suing. But in reality, it is the insurance company you are going after. The insurance company took the premiums, and they are supposed to pay for any judgment awarded to you. That nice man who hit your car from behind or that teenage grocery store clerk who forgot to clean up the cooking oil spilled in aisle five—they are not the ones who pay. And there is always insurance in Ontario accidents.

You've suffered a terrible loss. Making someone else pay just *sounds* mean. And yes, it's going to be even more difficult if the person you are suing is a friend, or even a family member. Every time these thoughts cross your mind, remember: everyone pays monthly premiums for insurance—millions of dollars each year, an estimated $42.4 billion in 2020, according to the Insurance Bureau of Canada's 2021 fact report. And insurance companies in Canada invested $134.6 billion in assets in 2020 from the profits they made.

Front-loading your case: the secret behind setting reserves

One of the lesser-known strategies for getting a maximum dollar amount has to do with a practice called "setting reserves."

At the beginning of a case, the insurance company is required to set up a reserve amount of money so it is ready to pay out if the case goes to trial and a judgment is given. Determining the amount to reserve can be a challenge, given the limited amount of information the insurance company has at this stage about the accident and your injuries. The last thing an adjuster wants to do is set a reserve too high, but it is more than embarrassing if the reserve is set really low, and two years down the road, the amount required is triple what's been set aside. This spells serious trouble for the insurer.

For this reason, a good personal injury lawyer provides the adjuster with documentation about the claim and injuries, including medical records and photos, as soon as possible. This actually helps the adjuster set the right amount. Better still for you, front-loading the case in this way influences how the reserve is set.

You won't know that this is happening, but you will notice in our first meeting that we collect and ask for as many documents as possible, even before a lawsuit has begun. It's all part of how we front-load your case in order to influence the reserve amount—the higher the reserve, the better the chances of obtaining a good settlement offer later down the road.

You can have fast or fair, but not both

A final word on insurance: be prepared for a lot of waiting.

Dealing with insurance companies is a long and often demoralizing process, and it continues through all the stages of litigation. Each time a settlement offer is made by our side, a response from the insurance adjuster can take weeks to arrive, and when it does, the amount could be way too low. The average overworked adjuster carries over 100 cases, which doesn't help. And remember: the insurance company doesn't work for you or even their policy holder: they work for their shareholders and their own profits. If you get discouraged and give up, that is okay with them. In fact, they're delighted!

As your personal injury lawyers, we will support you, talk you through the tough times, and remind you of our goal and mission when you feel your patience might be waning. We are going to continue to build your case—that's the real magic to getting you a favourable result regardless of the time it takes.

5

Building a Case with Finesse: Not Your Average Desk Job

LING WAS a sprightly octogenarian. He broke his arm in a slip and fall caused by broken pavement. When it came to determining loss, Ling's injuries were assessed by the at-fault insurance adjuster on the basis of his age. How much difference was an injury going to make in Ling's life, given that he probably just sits around in his La-Z-Boy chair all day watching soccer?

Their assumptions about Ling were far from accurate. We suspected this when we first met him and realized he was not your average 80-year-old. Following a thorough investigation, including a visit to his home, we had evidence to prove it. Right before the accident, Ling had been a competitive runner, with shelves packed full of trophies celebrating past and recent successes. Ling wasn't out walking that day—he was in training!

By taking photos of these awards and presenting evidence of what Ling had actually lost, we were able to build Ling's case and settle with an award triple what the insurance company first offered. There is no substitute for a personalized approach to building a case.

BUILDING A case and dealing with insurance companies is about the evidence we gather and the picture we paint of a life-changing event. All of this information creates exposure to the insurance company, and this is what gives us the edge during settlement negotiations. By "exposure," we mean: What are the risks if this case—so well built—ends up at trial and the insurance company loses big? It could be exposed to the risk of a serious payout.

Unflinching negotiation skills are important for a personal injury lawyer, but for us, success rests on the case we build in the first place. The story of Ling reminds us that everyone has a story. Taking the time to understand someone's story is part of uncovering evidence to show someone's life before an accident, and what that person has truly lost after an accident. If we build the case well, we can make it very difficult for an insurance company to risk taking it all the way to trial.

Insurance companies are large corporations, with shareholders to please and profits they want to invest. They don't care about Ling or his story, or even the before and after. They care about losing money because of a bad risk assessment.

To go to trial or not to go to trial?

Before we go too far along, we need to be clear about something. Even though we build your case as if it's going to trial, our goal (and your goal) should be to settle before a trial. This is often a surprise to people. Court scenes in movies are where all the excitement happens. The lawyer (played by your favourite movie star) fights for the deserving victim and brings the other side to their knees, begging them to take their money.

It doesn't usually happen that way. Only about 5 percent of cases in Ontario ever go to trial. And that's a good thing. If we can get you a fair settlement without a trial, that's what we want.

Most personal injury cases are heard by juries, which generally are not good for our side. This is in part because the laws of evidence and rules of procedures dictate that various secrets are kept from the jury. For example, in a car accident case, jurors cannot be told that there is an insurance company defending the at-fault driver and paying out any judgment. Often jurors are thinking that a poor (albeit negligent) driver will be left paying a large amount when that is virtually never the case. That's just one of many secrets that prevent the jury from getting all the information they need.

Plus, there's the time factor. Think about how much you want this all behind you. There is a huge backlog in Ontario to get a trial date, so it means waiting two to three years. That adds a risk element in addition to the frustration of waiting. Maybe something will change in your condition or your life circumstances. If we get a deal done now, you can finally get on with your life, cheque in hand.

So, what really happened?

The day we're first hired, we begin building your case as if it will go to trial. (There are milestones along the way where a settlement could be reached—we'll talk about them in later chapters.)

Our process starts by looking at what we need to prove in two areas:

1 Who is responsible for your injuries (fault)?

2 What are the losses (medical, financial, psychological, personal, etc.), now and in the future?

We are thorough as we put together the pieces starting from day one. For example, surveillance footage at the scene shows that you had the right of way when you made your turn—this backs up who's at fault. Expert opinion from a neurosurgeon explains why your injuries are going to make it impossible for you to return to your job—this speaks to losses.

Determining fault

Determining fault is all about finding out what really happened, beyond the police report. We gather evidence in various ways. Some of it is detective work, carried out by an actual private investigator.

Our work includes visiting the scene, collecting and reviewing witness statements, taking photos, looking at surveillance videos and traffic signal records from the time of the accident, and going to court if we need to get further records from the police. When needed, we'll bring in biomechanical engineers to do accident reconstruction. If there is an event recorder chip in a vehicle's airbags, we'll get the data from those recordings.

The following examples show how this works:

- You recall that right before your accident, the light was green, but the driver and a passenger witness on the other side claim it was red. We can retrieve the traffic signal information from the municipality about the sequence of the lights at the time and date of the accident. Argument put to rest.

- You slipped and fell in a grocery store. You are sure that the floor was damp when you fell. The store manager, however, says, "Come on, where would the water come from anyway?" Our private detective visits the store and finds out that the freezer nearby has a slow leak. Now we know.

Determining damages

When building a case for damages, we look at your life before and after the accident. This is how we show that your life has been changed very significantly. Before the accident, you were able to live a certain way and earn a living because of your skills and abilities; after the accident, many aspects of living and working are no longer possible for you. We build your case in this way by hiring medical experts to give us evidence on permanent impairments, long-term functional problems, or medical needs into the future. We also gather work records and income tax returns, and we hire forensic accountants to estimate your future losses. Some of the very best evidence comes from friends, relatives, co-workers, and neighbours who can describe the changes they see in you because of the accident.

The insurance company, of course, is going to look for ways to minimize or deny our "before and after pictures" as a way to minimize or deny the damages. For instance, if you experience chronic pain as a result of your injuries, the insurance defence lawyer might deny that your pain is caused by the accident and look instead to pin it on a pre-existing condition, perhaps trauma from your past or a condition such as fibromyalgia.

Proving that symptoms and impairments are a direct result of an accident is not straightforward, despite the fact that it is very clear to you that the pain keeping you up at night is new. This is why it's so important to hire expert medical witnesses (see Chapter 10 on medical assessments) who can speak to the injuries sustained in your accident and the fact that the accident actually caused these injuries.

When determining losses, here's the kind of evidence and documentation we gather to determine the extent of your injuries, how they were caused, and what they mean in terms of future losses.

Success rests on
**the case we build
in the first place.**

Medical and rehabilitation records

Beginning from your first emergency hospital visit, we look at medical and rehabilitation records, such as X-rays, tests, surgeries, doctors' visit notes, therapies, interventions, medications, and alternative therapies.

Check out the following examples:

* You've been seriously injured after heavy items from a top shelf in a store fell on your head (yes, it happens). While at some point you'll be able to return to work, your life has changed in a big way. It's now unlikely that you'll get that promotion you were working toward before the accident. We hire a forensic accountant, who examines your employment and income records in order to assess your future earning potential and calculate economic losses over a lifetime. Now we have a defensible account of your future income losses.

* It's been a year and a half since your accident and you are not recovering well. The insurance company defence lawyer is arguing that your accident was not serious enough to cause the painful disc bulge, which is causing such pain and dysfunction. It's time for an expert opinion. We hire a biomechanical engineer as well as an accident reconstruction engineer who sets up a reconstruction of the accident in order to determine the force that was exerted on your body. We bring in an orthopaedic doctor to verify the damage done to your back. Turns out, the impact was clearly enough to cause serious, long-term damage, and the damage was a direct result of the impact. Point made.

All of this means that a typical day-in-the-life at our firm does not involve us sitting behind a desk. A lot of the work takes place outside our office, investigating details related to your accident—everything from visiting the scene of the accident to filming the traffic flow at the curve where the accident happened. We use an expert private investigator to interview every person who witnessed the accident. Often, we hire an accident reconstruction expert to study the case so victims receive fair compensation. Whether or not these activities and research are all done by a lawyer, a student, a paralegal, or a hired private detective, every piece of information and evidence we collect is examined in terms of how it could impact the value of your case.

Your role in gathering records

You have a starring role in building the case too. There may be records we need that require your permission for us to ask for them. We'll want to interview people who can talk about how the accident changed you in terms of ability, skills, and even personality—and you can help us find the right people and ask them to help.

School records

For a child or a young person in their early to mid-20s, we may collect Ontario school records from the last school attended, as well as university and college transcripts, certificates, and diplomas. We do this to get a picture of someone's strengths and weaknesses as they apply to the workforce. For example, imagine that a young person working in a high-paying construction job suffers serious physical injuries. He had done very well in his job but now won't be able to do work that requires physical labour. If that young person's academic record shows learning disabilities or academic struggles, we will be able to show that he can't just substitute a desk job. His income losses will be larger and it's his report cards that will help us prove it.

Employment records

We'll need to have a picture of what you used to do in your job (and what you were paid) compared to what future work looks like for you. You may be reluctant to give us permission to access employment records because it also means telling your boss about what happened. Employment records, however, can be very valuable for building a good case. Although we do not tell the employer why we are asking for these without your permission to do so, it's usually best to say why, so your boss isn't left wondering what's going on. We will probably want the records from all or most of the jobs you have held.

Witnesses, personal and at work

We'll ask for names and contact information for witnesses who know you (such as family members) and workplace witnesses. We'll interview as many of them as you give us. You are never forced to give us names, but these interviews are critical for supporting a maximum settlement.

These are the people who can really paint a picture of how your injuries have caused life-altering changes. They can speak about your demeanour and your ability to focus, communicate, or remember details before the accident compared to now. There may be an obvious memory or physical change, or something in your personality, that someone who worked with you can speak to honestly.

This is another challenging area. After all, who wants their co-workers to know that they can no longer do their job? The same applies to business owners and their clients. Keep in mind, workplace witnesses who can speak to how you've lost your competitive advantage are the hardest to find, but they are also the most effective in building a strong case. Particularly in the eyes of a judge or jury, co-workers are considered much more objective than family.

Keeping us up-to-date

Our record gathering continues as new or updated information is added. Medical care and visits covered by OHIP are available to us, but we need you to keep us updated on other treatments you are receiving (and paying for), such as acupuncture, naturopathy, physiotherapy, massage therapy, chiropractic therapy, yoga therapy, or occupational therapy.

You missed an appointment? Not a good idea

Records that indicate you were a "no show" at a medical or rehab appointment do not look good when we are arguing your case—regardless of your reason. If you do not go to your treatments or don't take the medicine prescribed, you are sending the message that "things must not be too bad, after all she's able to skip her pain medication and not show up at physio."

We get that you may not want to take all the medication prescribed to you. Many people have understandable concerns about side effects and addiction. Talk with us so we can at least present an alternative plan. Perhaps you cut back on your medication and set up a drug-free pain management routine each night that will work well for you. We'll help you address this issue when it comes up. (Yes, it will come up.)

CASE STUDY: Finesse is in the details

Several years ago, we had a case where a woman fell down the stairs at a grocery store. She was being careful. She had her hand on the railing, but when she slipped, she wasn't able to catch herself before she tumbled.

You have a starring role in building the case too.

The defence, of course, said it was her fault; she was just clumsy. Our firm, however, wanted to figure out what had really happened. We knew from experience that hand railings aren't always built to *Ontario Building Code* standards. The *Code* is very specific. It states, for instance, the diameter required for a proper grip and it varies by the actual shape of the railing. Other factors include the height above the floor and the minimum distance from the wall.

The only way to know for sure was to go to the site. Off we went, measuring tape and camera in hand. It turned out that the railing, a new one built in 1996, was not up to code. No wonder the woman couldn't properly hang on to stop her fall. As a result of our case, non-compliant railings in that chain of stores all over the province had to be changed.

Wow, didn't realize you guys were so busy

Covering off these details may seem obvious, but not all personal injury firms are meticulous. Remember the 20-cents-on-the-dollar lawyer? That lawyer only collects the police report from the collision, and that's about the end of it.

Be patient through this phase. It feels like a lot of digging around; we agree, and it's going to take a while. Most of this evidence building occurs while you get on with your rehabilitation and recovery. Although there's not much you need to do except keep us updated (we'll call you every few months to make this happen), know that there's a lot of activity going on.

How we build your case ties in with how we assess the value of a settlement in dollars. It's a question we know you may have already asked!

CASE STUDY: The value of the before and after

Sarah and her young son were crossing the street on a green light when they were hit by a large truck. Sarah's son was fine, but Sarah's injuries were catastrophic, including a traumatic brain injury. Her story is an example of how a before and an after picture are core to building a case.

Before the accident, Sarah was a busy young mother with big plans for her future. She was finishing a few high-school credits so she could attend college and learn a profession. Life was full of possibilities. After the accident, everything changed. During her rehabilitation, Sarah required 24-hour care while she learned to walk and talk again. Although she completed her high-school diploma, a college program was no longer possible. This was another tough reality of her after picture.

To help build Sarah's case, we hired experts to calculate her economic losses, both immediate in terms of care and long-term in how her income would be affected since her ability to earn a living was significantly compromised. Evidence from her high-school program proved that Sarah had mapped out a plan for her future, so we were able to help project her loss of income. The result was a strong settlement for Sarah that is helping her manage the rest of her life.

6

The Numbers: What's Your Case Worth?

"SO, WHAT'S my case worth?"

This is one of the questions we hear right from the first phone call. You are right to ask it. The answer is not a secret. Once your lawyer starts building your case, we should be able to tell you what it's worth, and why. For instance, let's say we tell you that it's worth $70,000. We'll follow up with a synopsis of the cases we're relying on to estimate that number: which ones are more serious than yours and which sound less serious, and where we think your damages fall.

Unfortunately, you can't wish your way into a big settlement. Research and experience are required to properly value your case and look for ways to increase the award; there are negotiating skills required to argue the case from a position of strength; and finally there's finesse required to recognize the best time to propose a settlement.

Here's how we do this for you, beginning with the assessment of general damages.

Pain and suffering: general damages

The first item in a settlement and the first amount of compensation claimed in a case is the award for "pain, suffering, and loss of enjoyment of life," also known as "general damages."

All the pain and suffering damages are capped in Ontario at approximately $400,000 (indexed for inflation). There's no more money available, not even for a catastrophic injury or fatality. The only cases where claims get close to this cap are the most serious brain and/or spinal cord injuries or similar.

We determine the value of your case by looking at what judges have decided in cases similar to yours. The calculation of damages for pain and suffering in Ontario is not an exact science. The amount that a particular injury is worth (say, a torn rotator cuff or soft-tissue injuries in the lower back) depends largely on what other judges' written decisions have said it's worth.

We start researching case law (written decisions that only a lawyer could love).

Assuming there is a range of damages—and there usually is—we look for evidence that could push your case to the top of the range. For example, if a surgical resident was about to start her fellowship as a top surgeon and lost two fingers in an accident, the award might be greater than if either of us lawyers lost two fingers. We also uncover factors that could lower the number, so we can be honest with you about expectations.

An extra step for motor vehicle cases

After we figure out the range of damages, there is both a monetary threshold and a monetary deductible set by the *Insurance Act* that apply only to motor vehicle accidents.

If your injury attracts pain and suffering damages (that is, general damages) that are lower than the monetary threshold, a monetary deductible applies. Sometimes the deductible brings your pain and suffering damages to below zero. There is also a verbal threshold (discussed in Chapter 3) that requires the establishment of a serious and permanent injury.

All of these rules make things complicated. We'll spend time looking at how they impact the value of your case and clearly explain the reasons to you.

All the work we do means we can **negotiate with the insurance adjuster from a position of strength.**

There's no such thing as "blood money"

The amount paid in damages is intended to put you back where you would have been if you hadn't had the accident. The money is not intended to be a punishment. In fact, the person who caused your injury may never know the amount paid out by the insurance company. The money is not higher or lower depending on the severity of the defendant's negligence.

For many, this is very difficult to accept. It doesn't matter if the person was drunk while driving or just momentarily distracted—if the injuries are the same, so is the value of the claim. It doesn't make a difference how blameworthy someone was or how bad their driving.

Calculating the damages equation

We want your award to be as high as it can be. The damages equation we put together for you is the calculation of pain and suffering (or general damages) as a result of your accident *in addition to* other specific losses and damages.

We are serious about pursuing these additional losses and damages. The circumstances related to your particular case could mean that we pursue a claim related to loss of income, future medical care costs, housekeeping and attendant care claims, or any other type of appropriate compensation. In fact, in Ontario, the largest component of a settlement claim is typically made up of these additional items.

This is where both experience and perseverance come in. Not all law firms take on the work related to these claims. It requires a network of reputable experts, as well as hours of time spent researching and collecting records, witness state-ments, appointment information, and so on as evidence. The results of this effort are documents we can use before or at trial that apply principles of science, math, and evidenced-based research to back up the value of your case.

Here are the categories we look at to add to the value of your case.

Out-of-pocket damages or economic loss

Every time you have a medical appointment, you likely pay for parking or bus fare! Recovering from an accident-related injury and making it through months of trial preparation on a reduced income can be a strain on your bank account. The expenses you incur and the income you lose are often very significant components of your claim for compensation. As individual expenses, they may not seem like a lot of money, but they can add up over time. We'll make sure we calculate these for you—with your help.

Medical and rehabilitation expenses

Your injuries probably require health care services that aren't covered by OHIP, such as physiotherapy, occupational ther-apy, chiropractic and/or massage therapy, prescriptions, prolotherapy, psychology, vocational rehabilitation, dentistry, and in catastrophic cases additional services such as case management.

For motor vehicle cases, if you have extended health care benefits that cover all or some of these services, you will have to submit your expenses to that insurer first.

If you don't have extended health care, if there is a deduct-ible or an annual limit that you exceed, or if a particular service isn't covered, you'll have access to accident benefits insurance. If this is the case, we'll help make arrangements to have your services paid directly by the accident benefits insurer.

For cases that don't involve a motor vehicle, your extended health care insurance may ask us to claim repayment from the defendant from what they have paid out to you. It's called "subrogation." It's complicated! And we'll look after it for you.

Accident-related rehab services that are not covered by your own health care benefits can be claimed from the at-fault party. Again, these need to be tracked. In addition, there's a policy limit for accident benefits depending on the severity of the accident. We'll keep track of that as well.

Past and future loss of income

After an accident, the impact of your injuries could mean that you return to work but at a reduced capacity with less income, or that you can't return to work, which means no future income and, for many, the loss of pension benefits. Calculating loss of income during convalescence is straightforward. But what are provable predictions about the future, your future employability, and the potential reductions in your pension income?

For instance, if you had a salaried position but can no longer do the job, it is relatively easy to calculate your loss of income. However, we'll add into the calculation any raises or bonuses your co-workers received if you would have received the same. If you are retrained to work at another position, the income from your new position will have to be factored into your claim for losses.

Calculating loss of income is trickier when your pre-accident work was irregular, your career was on an upward trajectory, or market conditions in your position were changing. It is also more challenging to calculate income loss for people who are self-employed or receive tips or commissions. The quality of your future loss of income claim may be impacted by the quality of your pre-accident record-keeping. (If that's scary to you, we'll help as much as we can.)

What are provable predictions about the future, your future employability, and the potential reductions in your pension income?

These mathematical calculations are done by forensic accountants. We will also get medical opinions about your future employability and ask vocational experts to determine what other jobs you are qualified for, if any. The result is a strong, clear picture of what the accident has meant in terms of loss of future income.

Future care costs

Future care costs are particularly important for catastrophic injuries and/or injuries that have resulted in a permanent disability or chronic condition. These are care costs not covered by OHIP: everything from attendant care and chiropractic treatments to paying for wheelchairs and adaptive clothing.

We hire life care planners to create a comprehensive plan outlining the care you are expected to need as a result of the accident, for the rest of your life. As medical professionals with expertise in areas like psychiatry and rehabilitation, future care planners use a systematic approach to assess injuries and their impact. The reports they create include evidence-based research and dollar amounts to back up the claims.

Housekeeping claims

We will engage an occupational therapist (OT) to assess the impact of your accident on your ability to do your housekeeping and handyperson tasks at home. OTs are trained to assess the body mechanics needed to do particular tasks and can assign a time period it takes to perform those tasks. They can demonstrate, again through research, how specific injuries make it impossible to do certain (or all) housekeeping tasks—everything from shovelling snow and clearing the gutters to making dinners.

Housekeeping assessments are often conducted by occupational therapists who come in and observe you in your home. They assess what you cannot do and then determine how much time it would take for someone to complete those tasks for you.

Note that your share of housekeeping doesn't just fall to a spouse or someone else living in the home! It should be part of a fair settlement.

Attendant care claims

Attendant care is another category of future care. It includes daily assistance with activities such as bathing, dressing, and eating. If this applies in your case, a claim can be made for an in-home care attendant and/or convalescent care in a long-term care facility (not covered by OHIP). Your attendant care needs are also typically assessed by an occupational therapist.

Family Law Act claims

When people see the words *Family Law Act* in Ontario, they normally think of divorce and spousal support. While this act does deal with those issues, it also addresses the entitlement of certain family members to compensation for the loss of care, guidance, and companionship when a loved one is injured or dies. Let's face it, entire families are impacted by a serious accident. Someone has to drive or accompany the injured person to medical procedures and assessments. A spouse with a thriving career who becomes a major caregiver is no longer able to contribute as much to the family income. Even when a loved one is not involved in the direct care of their family member, they may still be eligible to claim damages for loss of companionship and guidance. All of these costs can be calculated and presented as part of a settlement claim.

Start writing stuff down

We encourage clients to keep a calendar of all their appointments and financial losses as a result of the accident. It's never too late to start. And don't underestimate the time and expenses. It all matters.

Perhaps you're unable to drive for four months because of a leg cast; you'll have transportation expenses. If you were driven by a loved one, a record of that person's time is important. Or you had to hire a babysitter to look after the kids because you can't take care of them due to your injuries or while you're at medical appointments, and you did not qualify for the caregiver benefit under the accident benefits. These are a few examples of the various kinds of expenses we are looking for when assessing the value of your case. Receipts make a big difference. We urge you to keep them.

What about damages when the injured person is a child?

We have secured very significant settlements for injured children. We've sued drivers, school boards, municipalities, and companies that have caused injuries to kids. Many of these cases are heartbreaking. But as parents ourselves, we put our emotions aside to secure the very best settlement and brightest future possible for injured children.

To maximize your child's financial recovery, we want to share some important advice. Most parents focus on the bright side when their kids are injured. They may not want to acknowledge that there's been a change in behaviour or academic achievement. Unfortunately, the desire to paint a positive picture can undermine your child's claim for damages. In some situations, it can also stall the rehabilitation process. The changes to your child and the needs of your child may not be well documented—and worse, the child may not receive the psychological or additional care they need.

Similarly, some parents do not tell the child's school about an accident, or they minimize the impact on the child. You may do this with the best of intentions to help the child get back to normal as soon as possible. Again, the result can be that important signals that the child is suffering are missed.

As parents ourselves, we can only imagine how difficult this is on you. We'll advise you on what actions and evidence are going to support your case, and what to avoid. For instance, when a child is injured, their school records are produced to the insurance defence lawyer. Teachers who know about the accident may want to encourage the child by painting a rosier picture than reality on the report card. On the other hand, teachers who do not know about the accident may treat a child who is suffering from post-accident woes as a troublemaker.

CASE STUDY: Someone to advocate for losses on your behalf

....

A settlement amount can look like a lot of money, but is it really enough to cover future financial losses because of a permanent impairment?

A few years ago, we had a case where an administrative assistant in a dentist's office broke her wrist in a fall. The long-term effect of the injury definitively impacted how well she could do her work. But her employer, a nice guy, continued to keep her employed at the same income level, even though she didn't have the same skill level as before the accident.

As her personal injury lawyers, we knew we had to advocate on her behalf in terms of future income. If she ever had to leave this particular employer (if he moved, closed his practice, retired!), her impairment would impact her ability to find another job or make the same kind of money.

How we negotiate your case (really well)

....

All the work we do to assess the value of your case means we can negotiate with the insurance adjuster from a position of strength.

Our tactics focus on skilled negotiation techniques:

- We go into negotiation with our target in mind. We are not unrealistic about the number. It is a goal we know we can justify based on the evidence we've gathered and the case law we've researched.

- We will encourage you to draw your "line in the sand." This is the number we won't go below without a fight (that is, going all the way to trial if necessary). You can be confident

What if the settlement amount isn't enough to cover the fees and expenses? Isn't that kind of a mess?

that we always have this number in our heads: if negotiations don't go well, we're not going to cave in on a low-ball number. (Unless you tell us to, which we know you won't.)

- We are very, very patient. Remember those settlement firms that based their business model on settling fast (and low)? That's not us. We are quite prepared to wait and reopen negotiations in a few months or wait for mediation or pre-trial. You get the picture.

- We never leave money on the table if we believe we can push for more.

- Timing is everything. In Chapter 13, you can read about the best times for settling and how we strategize on timing.

Whenever we suggest a settlement, we'll tell you what we are going to offer when we propose a settlement number and what we might expect from the other side. We'll also tell you what you will receive, after our fee and disbursements have been deducted. No secrets, no surprises.

Good reasons to feel confident

An obvious question may be "What if the settlement amount isn't enough to cover the fees and expenses? Isn't that kind of a mess?" Yes, it is a mess. And it happens—but not to us, and we won't let it happen to you.

Remember when we explained how sometimes we decline cases when we first meet a prospective client? We aren't shy about saying, "I'm sorry, but we can't help you," or being upfront about the fact that we don't think that the award would cover the deductible. By picking cases carefully, we are virtually always successful.

We're not looking to sign anyone on the other end of that first phone call. This is core to our business model. We screen every case from the first conversation, and the person taking the call is trained and experienced in doing initial assessments. We don't want to end up six or 18 months down the road with a best offer at $25,000 when we've already spent double that on disbursements. You don't want this either.

Likewise, throughout your case, we are assessing and reassessing. As new medical evidence comes in, we make sure we are still confident you will pass the threshold (in a motor vehicle case). If new liability evidence is presented, such as video of an accident scene, we make sure we are still on solid footing for liability. Trust us, if our feeling about the likely success of your case changes, we promise to tell you so that you are never put in a bad situation.

About those Facebook comments

You may have seen them: Facebook posts that say, "Stay away from personal injury lawyers because I got a settlement and it all went to lawyers' fees and expenses." That situation would *never* happen. First of all, in accordance with the *Solicitors Act*, lawyers that use a contingency agreement can never get more in fees than a client receives in a settlement. And second, if the entire settlement did get gobbled up with disbursements, we wouldn't receive any money either.

Getting to a good result

We are going to build up your case higher than anyone else might have done. By negotiating from such a position of strength, we expect to reach a fair settlement *and* avoid the risk of going to trial—which was our shared goal from the beginning.

The final settlement amount is likely not the number we started with in our opening offer. But the negotiated number we accept is going to be a good result. It will be worth all the time and effort we've spent (and you've spent). How can we be so sure? Because we would not have taken on your case if we didn't think so in the first place.

Look at an example. We hoped for $600,000. We settled for $500,000.

Was it worth the $100,000 we had to give up during negotiation? Yes, it was. If the case had gone to trial, trial expenses alone could be $100,000, plus the risk that if we lost, in addition to no money as compensation, there could be a cost award to the other side!

That's why we like to say that a good case is a settled case—not one settled quickly at a low-ball figure, but one that is assessed correctly, built up, and then negotiated in a way that makes sure no money is left on the table that could be directed toward helping you get your life back.

CASE STUDY: Our talent and advocacy for fair settlement is part of why we're here

There was one case in particular that Richard will always remember. It happened when he first worked at a large Bay Street firm, defending the "other side." The $50,000 settlement obtained by the defence was a good result for the multi-million-dollar insurance company—Richard's client at the time—but was not a good outcome for the family of the young person who'd been catastrophically injured in the accident. Richard couldn't get the case off his mind, so much so that he realized this was not the work he wanted to do, particularly with his own background growing up in a family where there had always been financial struggles in addition to health issues.

Once we set up our own personal injury firm, our experiences continued to reflect the way in which we both practice—and how we build a case and negotiate a favourable settlement for our clients:

- Never give up.

- Never take a low-ball settlement.

- Always push the envelope as far as you can in order to get the best outcome for the person experiencing real suffering.

7

Starting a Lawsuit: Let's Just Get On with It

THE PAST few months have been very difficult. You likely have felt stuck, unable to make any progress on getting your life back. Starting a lawsuit is going to help. Most people are ready for this step and actually look forward to things moving ahead, even though the word "sue" is now part of their world. Starting a lawsuit is an act of control. It is an assertive step at a time when control has eluded you. You've been the victim, the patient, the client—now finally you are taking a positive step on your own behalf.

Avoiding a lawsuit

Lawsuits don't start on day one after you retain our firm. In some circumstances, it makes sense to try to negotiate a settlement directly with the insurance company, which avoids a lawsuit altogether. This typically happens if you are recovering better than first expected. The injuries you sustained were severe, but now it looks like your before and after pictures aren't so different. If this is the situation, with your permission, we will send a demand letter to the insurance company that includes an amount that we would settle for.

Lawsuit on the horizon

Let's assume our demands made to the insurance company have not been met. It's now been a few months since your accident, and as we've continued to build your case, we're in a much better position to show that your injuries are still impacting your life in a significant manner. For instance, we may have notes from your employer indicating you tried to get back to work but couldn't manage, as well as medical updates that show there hasn't been much or any improvement. We also demonstrate that we've been reasonable in terms of what we expect in a settlement.

It's time to pull out all the stops and start a lawsuit.

How to sue in 70 words

In a lawsuit, as your lawyers, we have to prove not only that some-one was negligent but what the injuries are, the extent of these injuries, that the injuries were caused by the accident, and how they impact your ability to live, your future care costs, and your future income. We have to prove these elements on a balance of probabilities, referred to in legalese as the "burden of proof."

Who's who

During a lawsuit, the injured person who seeks compensation is referred to as the "plaintiff"—that's you. The person at fault is called the "defendant." We're the "lawyers for the plaintiff";

the insurance defence lawyer is hired by the insurance company to defend the person/entity at fault and the insurance company. We'll call them "the other side," "the insurance company defence lawyer," "the defence," or just "the bad guys."

Statement of Claim

The document in Ontario that starts a lawsuit is called a "Statement of Claim." The official form has two versions—simplified and ordinary—used for different monetary values of where the case might fall. A Statement of Claim is issued by the court and then served personally on the defendant (not their lawyers) by a process server. The Statement of Claim is accompanied by a letter from us that tells the defendant to pass it on to their insurance company.

We may issue a Statement of Claim while negotiating directly with the adjuster in order to show that we are serious. And we are serious. The message we are sending with this negotiation tactic is that this is the settlement amount we are looking for and we are prepared to proceed to a lawsuit if it is not met.

The court wants the Statement of Claim document to be terse and direct in tone. In it, we are asked to describe what happened and the negligence of the defendant, identify all the injuries and losses you have suffered (physical and psychological), and name the city where we want the trial to take place.

A monetary value is written on the Statement of Claim but it is usually only a placeholder, to cover the top end of the award scale. We don't yet know the value we will ultimately be asking for and there is strategy being exercised in terms of what we put down (so don't get attached to the number—it will change).

You'll be part of the process as we write the Statement of Claim line by line: how the accident happened, what the exact injuries were, and so on. You'll also be required to approve it.

The document is then issued by the court (electronically). We hire a process server, who delivers it personally to the defendant with a letter explaining what is happening. A courtesy copy is also sent to the insurance company to let them know that the individual they've insured is being sued.

Where's the beef?

Warning: a Statement of Claim is a bit underwhelming. It doesn't get into specific evidence with phrases such as "according to the police report or medical records." It mostly contains information we've covered from the beginning. This isn't an oversight. There are strict rules governing these documents. We're only allowed to state facts and at this stage our job is to be thorough and not miss anything. But take heart: if we proceed to the next steps, discovery and mediation, we'll get the chance to tell your full story.

Being served is not a pleasant experience, but it's done professionally. Once the defendant receives the document, they turn it over to their insurance company. The company defends and indemnifies them—which means the insurance company takes on the responsibility for paying and managing the file—and hires a lawyer to represent the defendant (under the instruction of the defendant's insurance company).

What if your brother (or friend or aunt or mother) is the at-fault driver and is being sued? Let him know so he hears

Starting a lawsuit is an act of control. It is an assertive step at a time when control has eluded you.

it from you first. The Statement of Claim will be delivered to
him in a humane manner (some scary bully isn't going to show
up at his door) and all he'll need to do is hand everything over
to his insurer.

Timeline: hurry up and wait

More patience is required once the Statement of Claim is filed.
The process is supposed to take 20 days, but it is rarely (i.e.,
never) that fast. By the time the document is served and the
insurance company responds, three or four months could pass.

When the insurance company *does* respond, sit down before
reading what you've received (perhaps make yourself some
chamomile tea). The other side is going to deny everything.
That's how the system works. They'll say everything—the
accident, injuries, losses—is a figment of your imagination.
Even when injuries are very serious, a typical response is that
the claim doesn't reach the threshold required, so go away.

We take this all in stride—you have to. There's lots of work
for us to do to keep building our case and that's what we focus
on. We'll update our medical files every six months, unless
you've undergone something like surgery and we want a
more current record. During this time, we also start scheduling the various stages of litigation. These follow in the next
chapters: examination for discovery, independent medical
exams, mediation, the pre-trial, and the trial.

What about my privacy?

Although the Statement of Claim is written to support a fair value in your case, the contents aren't pretty. It catalogues the seriousness of your injuries and the catastrophic loss that's happened to you—physically and psychologically. There is no doubt that seeing the list of your injuries and their consequences can be quite upsetting, particularly when they relate to issues related to appearance, ability to think clearly, sexuality, or a criminal proceeding.

Once the Statement of Claim is filed, it becomes a public document. If someone, like an eager beaver reporter, wants to dig into the details, they can. We've seen this happen, for example, when working on a highly publicized bus accident in the Ottawa area.

That's why, in certain circumstances, some clients agree to settle instead of pursuing a lawsuit. The money you receive will most likely be less, but the loss may be worth it in terms of securing your privacy.

If you do not want all the details captured in a Statement of Claim, we will respect your wishes and work toward the best settlement possible without a lawsuit. In special cases, we have had success in getting a court order protecting the identity and private information of the client, but this is rare and unusual for the court to order. The justice system operates on the principle of openness and transparency.

8

Discovery: Transforming You into the Best, Most Authentic, Honest and Accurate Witness

BRENDA STARTED her legal career on Bay Street with a large firm that represented corporate clients. In her second year, she was handed a cluster of files to prosecute on behalf of a bank. It was a real honour to be trusted with such an assignment. But the thrill of the work soon fell away. Brenda found herself part of a defence team denying mortgage insurance claims for widows. From the banks' point of view, the husbands had lied about pre-existing medical conditions or had habits such as smoking, which left them vulnerable to illness.

"There I was," she recalls, "sitting across from these women at discovery and asking questions but feeling great discomfort. It was the moment for me when I knew I had to find a way to exit and work for the other side."

Within six months, Brenda had a job at a smaller firm, working for people suing an insurance company, not losing to one. A few years later, she and Richard set up Auger Hollingsworth as a dedicated, compassionate personal injury law firm.

UNLESS THEY are settled first, most lawsuits include a meeting called "examination for discovery" (or "discovery" for short). At discovery, the lawyer (or lawyers) for the other side meets you for the first time and asks you questions directly; you have to answer without us intervening. Sound stressful? It can be. But preparing you for discovery speaks to why we got into the personal injury field in the first place—both of us chose to work on behalf of plaintiffs because we know how the process works, and we want it to work for you, not for the other side.

To be blunt (and we have to be at this point), discovery isn't fun. It's also pretty much the most important day in the whole case. If it doesn't go well, we'll likely have to settle for less. We're going to make sure it goes well. It's why we make preparation such a priority.

The time we spend ahead of time with you isn't just a nice talk over coffee. It's training and practice designed to help you be the best, most truthful, most accurate witness you can be. By the time the day of discovery arrives, you are going to be so knowledgeable and ready that we know you are going to do well. We also work with you to help build your confidence so that you are not nervous and so that you can tell your story.

What discovery is and isn't

The basic purpose of an examination for discovery is to allow each party and their lawyers to learn about and understand the other side's case.

Discovery sounds like a trial but is not. There is no judge, no courtroom, and you don't have to wait two to three years to schedule a date. However, you are under oath and what you say is sworn testimony, and the entire examination is recorded by a court reporter in a transcript.

Through their questioning, the lawyers for each party will try to learn a few basic things, including:

- The other party's point of view, by more fully defining and narrowing the issues

- If there are any areas where both parties are in agreement, which possibly allows for a pre-trial settlement

- An admission from the other party that later can be used in their client's favour while at trial (this is why preparation on your part is so important!)

Starting the discovery process: exchange of documents

The process starts with the exchange of documents. That's our task.

In any personal injury case, both sides have an obligation to release all relevant documents "under their power or control." As a client, you've already signed authorizations so we make these requests on your behalf. We prefer it this way, especially when it comes to medical records. If we can't find something, we'll ask for your help.

Our list is long and comprehensive, which surprises many clients at this stage. We are not overdoing it—just being thorough in how we build your case. Here's a small sample:

- All medical records (five years pre-accident and post-accident)

- Anything related to the accident itself, e.g., the police report and any ticket (if the person received one), photographs from the scene, receipts (for anything from repairs to property damage), records about road or walkway maintenance, a business card from a tow truck, the clothes that were soiled when you fell on a patch of oily pavement, etc.

- Documents related to the car itself or damage to the car

The basic purpose of an examination for discovery is **to allow each party and their lawyers to learn about and understand the other side's case.**

- Income tax returns, employment files, payroll files for claiming an income loss, documents that support missed opportunities for promotion and/or what future income is now lost

- Documents that could support other losses, such as medical expenses that weren't paid for by another insurance company; parking receipts; receipts for a cast, cane, or crutches; and prescription costs not covered by other benefit plans

- Records from your accident benefit insurer if it is a motor vehicle accident

We then organize your documents into a package called an Affidavit of Documents. This includes a list of "privileged" information—documents that need to be listed but whose content is not revealed, such as witness statements.

The defence does the same. It's usually a much smaller pile, containing property damage reports and other information relating to the insurance company's investigation of your claim. For a car accident, these documents could be related to the damage to the vehicle and photos from the scene. For a slip and fall, documents and records would be related to property maintenance and perhaps weather reports.

Leave the chasing to us—it's what we do

Both parties are supposed to review the Affidavit of Documents before discovery takes place. We send ours 30 days ahead. Typically, the defence doesn't. It is not unusual for us to have to chase down the other side.

Unlike some firms, we place a priority on getting these documents read in advance. It protects us, and you, from nasty surprises. You are entitled to know what they have as evidence ahead of time.

The big day

On the "big day," you first are asked to take an oath. You can do so by swearing on your choice of religious book or taking an affirmation that is "binding on your conscience."

You are there with your lawyer and the insurance company's lawyer, either in person or at a virtual discovery.

First warning: the defence may make small talk. Don't fall for it. You don't have to answer questions that aren't part of the official process. The best way to avoid small talk with the defence lawyer is not to be alone together. If you find yourself in that situation, leave and wait for your lawyer to enter the room.

Then the defence will start asking the official questions. It's likely that you'll get frustrated about how mundane these are. You may think, "Why are they asking me this? It's already in the medical records or the police records. Do we have to go over it again?" Second warning: be patient. Stay calm. It's all part of the process.

Showing frustration or getting snappy can hurt you at discovery. The insurance company defence lawyer is allowed to ask all the questions they want related to the case, if they are relevant, even if the answers are already in documents they have.

The questions

....

The order of the questions is controlled by the defence, but through experience, we know what's going to be asked when and how it will be asked. At first, there may be a lot about your home, in terms of the number or rooms, staircases, etc. We find these questions annoying. You will too.

Next come questions about your education and work history. It's a good practice to look at your resumé ahead of time so this information easily rolls off your tongue. Don't let these questions make you feel defensive or judged. Believe us, we've worked with clients from every walk of life. What we know for sure is that a fancy university degree isn't what makes you successful at discovery. All you have to be is genuine, straightforward, and truthful.

Then there are questions about your injuries, typically expressed in terms of "Tell me about your injuries, head to toe." You'll be asked about the treatments you've received for each—chiropractic, occupational, and physical therapy; what doctors and therapists you saw; and so on. For every medical person you met with concerning injuries related to your accident, you'll be asked how often you went, what they told you, and why you stopped going (if you did).

Another warning: questions about the actual accident often come at the end of the discovery, when you may be tired. Tell the lawyer if you need a break. You don't want to be answering important questions when your pain medication is wearing off or you are too tired to remember the details.

At the end of the examination, a transcript is prepared that gives a verbatim version of what was said at discovery. We may decide to order the transcript, or not, depending on the circumstances. However, if there is a trial pending, we will order it for sure. It gives you a chance to read it first and make any corrections in what you said. If you need to make corrections, you will tell us and we will write a letter to the defence lawyer.

What kind of witness will you be?

That all may sound fairly straightforward. Now it's time to look behind the curtain and find out what is really going on during discovery.

Discovery is when the other side first forms an impression of the strength of your case. The defence lawyer who questions you is the eyes and ears of the insurance company that is going to pay (or not). There are two areas they are assessing:

1   The factual content revealed at discovery: what is actually said and recorded in the transcript. All of this is now available to both sides to assess the strength of the facts. The transcript will be used if the case goes to trial.

2   Your strength as a witness: they are sizing you up in order to assess "Will we be able to use the discovery transcript to highlight inconsistencies in this person's storytelling and suggest to the court that they are not a credible (honest) witness?"

Consider the two scenarios that follow. Imagine what happens once discovery is over and the defence lawyer returns to his office and writes a letter to the insurance company and their client. Which scenario do you prefer?

"I examined Mary Smith today. Ms. Smith comes across as a credible witness, who has serious injuries. She is good at describing her injuries and her treatments since the accident. She's very straightforward with her answers. Given her overall honesty and likability, and the fact that her answers during

Discovery is when the other side **first forms an impression of the strength of your case.**

discovery were consistent with the records we have received, I would not recommend that we take this case to trial."

"I examined Harry B. today, and in our judgment, this is an individual who clearly would not present well at a trial. He is an exaggerator, to the point of coming across as a liar. When asked follow-up questions, he becomes difficult, even combative. On more than one occasion, he contradicted what was in his record or seemed confused about his past medical history. We don't think he is believable and suspect that a jury would feel the same way."

Be prepared

We're going to do our best to make sure you come across like Mary.

About one month before discovery, we hold two preparation sessions, two hours each. Ahead of the first session, you'll receive various resources and guides about the process, the rules, tips on how to prepare for potential questions, and what to watch out for.

Answering questions about past medical records is where most people get tripped up. We'll send the medical records we've collected ahead of time, so you have time to read them before our meeting. These are hard to get through—they're medical records, after all, written in medical language (at least these days most aren't handwritten!). But it's important to review them, especially the orthopaedic and emergency room ones so you can tell us if we are missing any information or details.

Then we'll spend our first session reviewing these records so that you can recall and talk about what's in each one, without contradicting yourself. It's not a memory test. For instance, you can always say, "I don't remember." But it looks bad if something is written in your medical record from two years before the accident, and you say, "That never happened." Okay, perhaps you had a minor surgery that you don't think is important (or you think you need to hide). Doing that is wrong and will hurt your case.

About those skeletons in the closet

There may be medical information you wish wasn't disclosed, perhaps pain from a pre-existing condition or records related to an addiction or personal issue. That's okay. We don't want to hide anything (and we don't want you to either!). Remember, being exposed as untruthful will damage your case. This is why, during our prep sessions, we'll talk with you about how to manage any "skeletons." Often a little context is all that is needed.

The same applies to your employment record. If you were reprimanded at work, you can't deny at discovery that it happened. However, during preparation, we can help you think about the context of the reprimand so that you can be forthright but also fair to yourself. And, by the way, people with skeletons in their closets are just as entitled to fair compensation as those without. (Most people have something in their past that they'd rather not share.)

Often records are helpful, even those you wish weren't there. Records that you wish weren't there sometimes help to explain why, say, your snowmobiling accident was so debilitating. Maybe the reason your shoulder is so messed up from the accident is that three years ago you had a shoulder injury. This doesn't necessarily diminish your claim. It speaks to why the injury is worse for you than for someone else.

It hurts "here"

A lot of people describe pain by pointing to where it hurts. Pointing doesn't come across well on a written transcript. It's much better to learn how to describe the location of the pain, e.g., "It's on my left shoulder, halfway between the edge of my arm, and then radiating to my neck."

The same applies to learning the best words to use. We can give you a hundred ways to describe pain because we've been using them for 20 years. But finding the right terms and phrases can be difficult when you're not used to talking about these things.

We often hear someone say that they have "discomfort." Is that really the best description? Discomfort sounds pretty mild. If you are unable to work because of "discomfort," then discomfort is the wrong word.

This is why, during preparation, we go over what body parts were hurt, help you think about the words to use, and practice using them.

A lot of people describe pain by pointing to where it hurts. **Pointing doesn't come across well on a written transcript.**

- Is it radiating pain, sharp pain, or intense pain? Does it throb? Does it ache? Does it make you cry out loud?

- Think of each injury in terms of the condition. Are there things you can't do now, such as crouching, reaching forward, or kneeling? What injury keeps you from sleeping at night because every time you roll over, a sharp, deep pain wakes you up?

There are added benefits to learning these terms. The better you are at describing what you really mean when you say, "My back is bothering me," the better you'll be at getting the right medical attention.

Finding the right words also applies to how you describe the accident. Most struggle to describe what happened because, face it, who goes through life talking about "curbside lanes" and "unassumed roadways"? By looking at diagrams, we'll help you find the right way to talk about what happened, e.g., "I was cycling in the curbside lane and then signalled that I was planning to turn right . . ."

We help you articulate your own story. We never tell someone to change the truth, but we do help them find the words to say what they want to say.

Discovery: what you need to know

WHEN? We'll let you know the date and the time.

HOW? Once a date is agreed on, we serve a Notice of Examination to the Defence (that is, we send a notice that requires they attend).

WHERE? An office boardroom or hotel conference room booked in the county where you live. If the meeting is virtual, we will send you the link to attend.

WHO WILL ATTEND? The plaintiff (you), the lawyers, and a court reporter. If there are several defendants, their lawyers. You can also request a translator.

HOW LONG? Three hours max for cases under simplified rules, seven hours max for regular cases.

ARE THERE BREAKS? Scheduled and requested breaks—for coffee, water, and yes, washrooms—and a lunch break (if it occurs over the lunch hour). Discovery can be stretched over two days.

WHAT'S THE DRESS CODE? Like you're attending your grandmother's funeral (depending on your grandmother)—be well groomed, presentable, and have no offensive slogans on your clothing.

What you cannot do at discovery

You knew it was coming: the dreaded list of what you cannot do at discovery:

- Once discovery starts, you aren't allowed to talk about the evidence with your own lawyer, even on a break, or turn to your lawyer for help. We don't even have lunch together because it could give the perception that we are talking about the case. You will never be left alone with the other side so there is no off-the-record chit-chat. We'll make sure you know to leave with one of us.

- You can't make small talk, not even things like, "Hey, what about the Raptors this year?" *Discoveries are not conversations.* They are formal, legal proceedings. Be polite, but don't make small talk.

- Don't fill empty air with words or "think out loud." Some people talk too much when they're trying to explain something; others say too little (and you likely know which type you are). If there is no question being asked, don't say anything.

- Don't oblige the defence by "fetching" something that isn't in their package of documents. For instance, the insurance company defence lawyer may ask for something we haven't given them, such as a certificate you've earned or a phone number of someone you mentioned. Leave it to us to answer the other side.

Here are things you can, and you should, do:

- Correct what you've said when you've misspoken.

- Ask for a break.

- Tell the defence if you don't understand the question or need it repeated.

- Expect to be treated with respect. The other side has to treat your professionally. They cannot badger you or be abusive. As your lawyers, we have the right to interfere, object, or stop the proceedings if this is happening. And we will do so!

You're not the only one answering questions

The defendant also has to answer questions at discovery—
questions posed by us as your lawyers. You are not in the room
at the same time, but you might see each other in the waiting
room if the examinations are back to back. If this is going to be
a problem for you, let us know. We can take steps so that you
don't see the defendant.

We ask the defendant for their version of how the accident
happened, as well as other questions related to damage/loss
and liability. It is a particular skill to know how to ask a question that brings out the right answer. Even in a situation where
the accident itself is not controversial, such as a rear-end
motor vehicle accident, we can get useful information from
the defendant about the force of the accident, the extent of
the damage to the car, and so on. For a slip and fall, we ask
about their maintenance protocols, maintenance records for
the past year, and so on.

You can be a discovery success

When it's your turn at discovery, you're bound to feel somewhat uneasy, knowing that you are going to be "on stage,"
where you have to sit in a strange boardroom, answer questions from the opposing lawyer under oath, and can't turn to
talk with your lawyer. In addition, all of this is held on a day
called "examination for discovery," with a list of don'ts such
as "don't contradict," "don't get frustrated," and "don't get
tricked."

None of this makes discovery sound like much fun (and
it's not).

We know the process can be very difficult to sit through.
This is why we spend so much time ahead of the day to help

you be the credible, straightforward witness that we know you can be. We have no doubt that we can get you ready. We are really good at it . . . just like you are going to be.

Can't you just tell me what to say?

When we are reviewing questions and answers with clients in preparation for discovery, it's common for a client to ask, "Can't you just tell me what to say?"

The answer is no, we can't. We have an ethical obligation to ensure your answers come from you—not us. We can't change your story. But as your advisor, we can help prepare you so that you can tell your story accurately and truthfully. For instance, we can look at what the record says (in past documents) and help you think about what you are going to say. We can help you work on the vocabulary so you have good words to use, and we can prepare you for what to expect. All of this is going to make you feel comfortable on the day, and perform your best.

9

Mediation: At Last, the Chance to Tell Your Story

SOMETHING TO look forward to in a lawsuit? You've got to be kidding. But it's true. Once discovery is behind you, most clients look forward to mediation—and for good reason. Mediation is the single day when your case is most likely to settle. There's a lot of reason for optimism.

The gap between sides is large when you start (otherwise, we would have settled by now). Every case has different positions on both sides in terms of liability (who's to blame), damage (the extent of the losses), and quantum (lawyer talk for the dollar amount of compensation, which is the settlement). But through mediation, we can bridge these differences until the gaps get small enough that we have an agreement, or at least an agreement in certain areas.

CASE STUDY: Bridging the gaps where we can

A few years ago, we had a tragic case where a 21-year-old was killed in a car accident. The fault was not in dispute. When both sides presented the case at mediation, it was fairly easy to close the gap in terms of damages from pain and suffering. We were able to agree on the dollar amount, which was close to the maximum cap for this category of award in Ontario.

Closing the gap for income loss was a different story. Overcome with grief, the victim's mother had not been able to

Through mediation, we can bridge these differences until the gaps get small enough that we have an agreement.

return to work since the accident, and the medical records we'd obtained backed up our claim that she would never work again. We therefore were asking for an additional amount to cover her loss of income. The defence totally denied the claim. This gap was too large to bridge, and when mediation failed, we set a court date.

Why mediation?

Mediation is an opportunity for both sides involved in the lawsuit to settle outside of court. The purpose of mediation is not to determine who wins and who loses but to develop creative solutions to disputes in a way that is not possible at a trial.

The mediator's job is to help the injured person (with their personal injury lawyer) negotiate with the insurance company and its lawyer in a constructive manner, to gain a better understanding of the interests of all parties, and to find a resolution based on common understanding and mutual agreement.

Mediation is mandatory in the most populated centres in Ontario under the Rules of Civil Procedure, and it's mandatory for car accident claims under the *Insurance Act*, if the person who was injured wants it. But even if the injury was caused by another kind of accident, for example a slip and fall, we often can convince the opposing side to participate in voluntary mediation.

Here come the briefs

Lawyers like to talk a lot about briefs. We know what you're thinking. But when we say "brief," we just mean a concisely written document that gets across information without using too many words.

Ahead of mediation, both sides prepare mediation briefs to tell their version of events to the mediator. This mediation brief, also called a statement of issues, is where we get to do the most thorough job telling our client's story. We talk about the accident, including maps and photos; we talk about the injuries, including snippets from the medical records. We almost always include before and after photos of the client. If there are legal issues in dispute, we'll also demonstrate how the law is on our side. It's a major undertaking for what we hope to be an optimal time to settle your case.

Although the rules say seven days, we prepare and deliver our defence brief to the defence 30 days before the mediation date. Not all firms are this proactive, but we do it sooner rather than later as part of our strategy for reaching a successful outcome. Our mediation brief gives the other side time to analyze the strength of the case we've built and the settlement we are proposing, and to ask themselves, "Does the plaintiff present a compelling case for compensation? If so, how much?" Our goal in the brief is to convince the insurance company, in advance, that they should settle on the day of mediation. A 30-day window also gives them enough time to determine the amount they are willing to pay and get the authority to make that decision on the day of mediation.

Going into mediation with your eyes open

The other side is supposed to send their mediation brief seven days in advance as well. This doesn't often happen. It typically arrives the day before or on the day of mediation.

Remember how you sat patiently during discovery, answered all the other lawyer's questions, and poured out your heart about the details of the accident and your injuries? Now you have a defence brief in your hands that gives an absolutely scathing report, perhaps calling you a liar and a faker, and making out that the accident didn't even happen.

We do need you to read this document before we start, and to try to keep it in perspective.

First of all, it's likely that document was put together by an articling student who wasn't even in the room when discovery took place. Our own view is that taking cheap shots at the injured plaintiffs in a document that is never tested in court is a cowardly act.

Second, there are always two sides to every story, and you do need to know what is being said about you and your case. The defence brief helps you see the case through someone else's eyes (even when you don't like what they see).

For instance, let's say you leaned on a broken railing and fell, suffering a serious head injury. Before the accident, you were up for two promotions, which you now cannot accept. The loss of these opportunities is going to have a big impact on your income, including a lower pension amount.

In response, the defence brief is going to give another side. They'll show your employment record as somewhat spotty, and to be honest, the facts are pretty clear to support this. Both of your performance reviews before the accident were negative, and even though you can name reasons why (e.g., the manager didn't like you), in the eyes of the defence, what matters is how a jury or judge would perceive this. Will they really think that someone with negative performance reviews was going to enjoy two promotions? Maybe yes, maybe no. But you have to accept the risk that they may not think so.

Some lawyers tell their clients to ignore the defence brief and just pretend to listen when it is read. We don't agree with that. It's very important to read the defence brief ahead of mediation, even when it is provided at the last minute.

What mediation looks like

Mediation is going to feel a lot different from discovery. There's no oath this time, no sworn testimony, no transcript, and no insurance company defence lawyer firing questions at you. We do all the talking and it's all about telling your side of the story. We also get to recommend the mediator (and usually get agreement on our choice), so we select from our list of very experienced mediators, picking one that we feel is ideal for the circumstances of your case.

Before we begin, the mediator makes some opening remarks. As lawyers for the injured person's side, we're up first. We usually do a spoken presentation, which takes anywhere from ten to 20 minutes. It can be an emotional ride, so be ready with the tissues. You'll hear us tell your story in a compelling manner—and we're good at it. Listening while we describe what you've lost and how your injuries have changed your life can be an emotional experience.

Next, the defence presents their side. This can be hard to hear. Some defence lawyers are quite effective and can make you nervous when they present your case. While it is important to listen to what they have to say, remember that words are not evidence, no matter how emphatically spoken! Clients are not expected to speak (most are very glad about that). We answer any questions that are asked, although if there is a clarifying question such as "Are you still in physio?" you may have to respond directly.

Sometimes we make offers in our opening remarks, but usually after the presentations, each side goes alone with their lawyer to a separate break-out room to talk money. Settlement offers are exchanged back and forth through the mediator. We make our offer first, and then we are countered by the defence.

As offers are made, the mediator passes on information such as whether or not we are "getting close," or if something in particular is causing an impasse. There's often a point when the mediator chooses to speak with one or the other lawyer separately without you in the room. This can happen when there may be a chance for negotiation on an issue that's important to the insurance company, or to us, but isn't a factor that affects the final number.

Be prepared by thinking about the numbers

The other part of preparation involves thinking about the numbers. We may have talked about settlement earlier in the process, but ahead of mediation, we will have a specific conversation on the subject.

You play a key role in the success of mediation.

As your lawyers, we'll make a recommendation as to the amount we think your case is worth and advise on what we believe should be the first offer. We discuss our recommendations ahead of the mediation so that you are not surprised by the number and have time to process what we are advising.

Where did that number come from?

Every case has to be analyzed as to its facts and circumstances. See Chapter 13, on settlements, to learn how we arrive at a settlement number.

How do the numbers get exchanged?

After the opening presentations, we are ushered into a private room together (or we are put in a private virtual room). We will have a chance to put any finishing touches on our opening offer before the mediator comes to see us. We will write the numbers down in front of you—it will be completely transparent—and you will let us know if you agree to make that offer.

The mediator will come into the room after a while and, assuming we are ready, we'll present our offer. Sometimes we explain the rationale for the numbers. Other times the basis is obvious. The mediator may have feedback on the offer. We welcome feedback because it is helpful to hear someone else's perspective. However, in the end the offer we make is up to us. (It's actually up to you!)

After the mediator leaves to deliver the offer to defence, we will have time to kill. For real. Sometimes it is 45 minutes before an offer comes back. If there are many parties, it can be even longer than that. During that time, you can use your phone, read a book, have a snack, get up and stretch, or all of the above. We will probably talk about what our next move will be while we wait for the mediator to return.

When the mediator returns to our room, we'll get the defence offer. Brace yourself. No matter what we tell you in advance, you will be shocked by the first offer. And not in a good way. First defence offers are notoriously low. You may feel insulted. It is not personal. We'll say it louder for the people in the back: IT IS NOT PERSONAL. Almost every single first offer we ever get at mediation is very, very low.

We will then make a counteroffer. Rinse and repeat. A successful mediation may have ten or more rounds of offers. As long as the defence is moving in the right direction, we will be patient and keep making offers, until we get close to (but not at) your final number.

When we get close to our final number, we will let the mediator know we don't have much room left to move. The mediator will convey this message to the defence. At that point, we'll probably get a message back (or an offer) that signals whether a deal is likely. Depending on how far apart we are, we will discuss various strategic options and decide what to do next. Sometimes we will make a final offer. Other times we might ask the mediator to try to broker a deal using one of the many tools available to mediators.

Shortly after that exchange, we'll know if we have a deal or not. If we do, there will be paperwork! If we don't, we've learned a lot about how the defence views your case and what areas we need to build further to get them to the numbers we need.

Numbers talked about at mediation stay at mediation

If mediation is not successful, the conversations that took place there are strictly confidential (no transcript). Any of the offers we made can't be brought up at a later day. For instance, if the case goes to trial, the $300,000 we offered as a settlement amount at mediation is no longer on the table. We can ask for more (and the defence knows that).

This is not magic—
**it's hard work
and experience.**

What's the magic to successful mediation?

Mediation happens over the course of one day. But the key to a successful outcome mainly rests on how well your case has been built up over months of research, investigation, and analysis. This is not magic—it's hard work and experience.

There is, however, some magic in the art and science of negotiation and the advocacy that goes along with these skills.

It helps—a lot—to have a lawyer who is perceived as some-one who would be a threat at trial. Insurance company defence lawyers and adjusters can recognize when you have a lawyer who will advocate your case in a convincing way to a judge and a jury. They take into consideration their experience with a given law firm, and whether that firm is likely to take a case all the way to trial. Imagine the defence considering two different types of personal injury lawyers:

> "Hmmm, I know the lawyers on this case. They are going to push us. Let's go to the mediation tomorrow with authori-zation to go as high as $300,000. We'll likely have to shell it all out to the plaintiff."

> "Who's the lawyer on that case? Ah, it's someone we haven't seen in court. That lawyer might not even go to court. Let's offer $10,000 at first and try to close for $50,000, even though we are authorized for $300,000."

Which situation would you prefer to see with your case?

What if we don't get
the number we want at mediation?

Sometimes, a client says to us, "I can't go past mediation—I just want this all over." This is your right. You are in charge and you give us instructions. If you want us to end the case on mediation day getting the highest amount we can that day, we will do that. However, we will tell you if we think you are leaving money on the table. We may urge you to consider going to pre-trial if we don't think the offer is all it can be. However, in the end, you will make the call.

Sometimes just a few days or weeks of patience can really pay off.

In a recent case, the final offer was $10,000 short of what we wanted. The other side was clear: they simply did not have authorization for more money. Our side was also clear: we were going to insist that they find that money. In the end, the insurer found a way to get about $6,000 more. It wasn't a lot of money, but hey, who wouldn't want an extra few thousand?

Do we have a deal?

Reaching a settlement at mediation sounds like a reason to celebrate, but most clients feel a little bit ambivalent about the whole process at the end of a long day—and that's understandable. First of all, you may be exhausted. But more importantly, a negotiated settlement means that both sides have had to compromise—there is no way around it. The sting of compromise may be greater right now than the joy of having all of this over with.

That's understandable too. But remember this: a settled case is a good case. What you've gone through, and what's been achieved, will sink in over time. Pretty much everyone feels good about the outcome the day the cheque arrives (see Chapter 14, Closing the Case).

If, on the other hand, there was no agreement, the mediator files a document with the court in your particular jurisdiction. We are now permitted, on your behalf, to set the case down for trial and set a pre-trial date. All is not lost at this stage! Mediation has laid the groundwork, and settlement discussions can continue and do—often with a good settlement taking place several weeks after mediation, when the other side sees the possibility of a trial getting closer.

Make no mistake: none of this is normal

As lawyers, we sometimes get desensitized to the process, but we understand that these steps in a lawsuit such as discovery and mediation are not normal in terms of how most of us behave with fellow human beings. For instance, let's say during discovery the defence lawyer from the insurance company has been pleasant to you. Then you receive a scathing mediation brief from the defence that accuses you of lying and faking. Next, you arrive at mediation, and that same lawyer is all sweetness and light again. It's understandable that you are going to find this difficult or incomprehensible. Take a deep breath and be reassured: this is just how these things sometimes go.

Don't get tricky on us

You play a key role in the success of mediation. Like you did at discovery, you do this by being yourself, not by playing someone you think that the mediator—or we—want to see.

This is not a time for a big show. Similar to discovery, mediation is a serious occasion where all we ask is that you be truthful and be yourself. The insurance adjuster and the defence are going to be assessing how well you conduct yourself, to determine how you'd come across if the case went to trial.

CASE STUDY: So, where did that walker come from?

A few years ago, we arrived at mediation and to our surprise and horror, our client showed up with a walker she'd borrowed from her neighbour. Her injuries almost a year earlier had been serious, but with treatment, she had now largely recovered—and there was a stack of medical records to prove so.

The drama was obvious to everyone in the room—in particular, the insurance adjuster. At no time through her recovery had she ever required a walker. None of the records had ever referred to such a device or an ongoing condition that would require it. It was just a prop she decided to add in for dramatic effect.

Needless to say, it did not go well for her. We only hope that the neighbour got her walker back.

THERE ARE other mistakes that we warn you about. For instance, if your injuries resulted in chronic back pain, don't show up in three-inch heels. If you've suffered a serious arm or shoulder injury, leave that giant purse or knapsack at home. Adjusters are trained to spot such inconsistencies.

However, do bring whatever you need to keep yourself comfortable for the day. Negotiations could go on for hours. Bring your pain medications, your ObusForme, a book—whatever you need so you can keep going or to fill up the time. Speak up if you are in pain, but don't think that you can fool the others in the room by exaggerating how you feel. And if you have ideas, such as using a cane even though you've never used one before, check with us first.

CASE STUDY: We can be pushy when it comes to getting you those extra dollars

There are times when mediation fails even though the parties aren't that far apart. The insurance company gives a "final offer," and we don't think it is good enough. In this situation, we might ask the insurance adjuster to go back for more authority. If the mediation has gone well, sometimes the adjuster will agree to do that, although it does depend on the insurance company's internal policies too.

We used this strategy in a recent case when faced with one such "final offer." We convinced the mediator to go back to the insurance defence lawyer with a number we could live with if we settled that day. Rather than drag the matter on for several more days, they agreed. We got the money.

Mediation: what you need to know

WHO WILL ATTEND? A mediator, you and your lawyer, the insurance adjuster, and the insurance company defence lawyer. If there are multiple claimants, the claimants and their lawyers.

WHEN? In most instances, mediation follows discovery. There are exceptions. When there's little or no debate about who is responsible, and the issue is about the damages amount, mediation can come first. In long-term disability cases, the insurance company will also agree to mediation before discovery. Municipalities also will agree to put mediation first.

WHERE? At our offices or a boardroom booked at a neutral location, e.g., a hotel or court reporter's office. Everyone sits together in the boardroom, and there are break-out rooms where each party and their lawyer(s) can meet separately. Or it could be online at a virtual mediation.

HOW LONG? It should be three hours; in reality, it often takes all day.

WHAT'S THE DRESS CODE? Like at discovery, be well groomed, presentable, and wear nothing offensive or too flashy. Leave the high heels and heavy handbags and knapsacks at home.

10

Independent Medical Assessments: Probably Not Your Favourite Part

L ET'S SAY you've always had back problems. In fact, in the years before the accident, you've seen a few back specialists, including an orthopaedic surgeon. She identified your condition as the result of degenerative changes, basically "wear and tear" on your spine. All of this happened before you were thrown from your bicycle after hitting a large pothole. Ever since the accident, you've been receiving treatments for whiplash, two damaged discs, and various soft-tissue injuries. The pain you're experiencing every day is so bad that you cannot return to work, and there's been no sign of improvement.

As your personal injury lawyers, we need to prove that the city, which is responsible for road maintenance, was at fault. It will be pretty straightforward. We also have to build a case for the extent of your injuries and how they are going to impact your life. That means gathering evidence through your existing medical records and an independent medical assessment in order to answer the question: Is the pain you are now suffering caused by the bicycle accident? Another way lawyers like to ask this question is: But for the bicycle accident, would you be able to work and do your activities of daily living?

These are not easy questions to answer.

Independent medical assessments are intended to provide an experienced, authoritative opinion about your diagnosis, the relationship between your diagnosis and the accident, what the future holds in terms of likely improvement, and what type of future care you will need as a result of the injuries. Depending on the case, we might also ask the expert to give an opinion about your ability to work or do housekeeping chores or perform childcare. It's not enough to just say someone can't work at their former job because their back hurts; we must provide evidence showing the extent of your injuries and precisely how those injuries are impacting your ability to live your life, go to work, and earn a living.

Why an independent medical exam is necessary in most motor vehicle cases

In the case of a car accident, there are specific questions required by law that must be answered in order to receive damages for pain and suffering. The major one is establishing a "permanent, serious disfigurement or a permanent serious impairment of an important physical, mental, or psychological function." Hiring an expert to assess you is an effective way to get answers to these questions.

Independent medical exams

Our firm places a lot of importance on independent medical exams. They are an extremely important part of a case where the injuries, and the consequences of those injuries, are ongoing.

Medical assessments can (and are) requested by both sides: we refer to ours as "independent medical exams" (IMEs) and the insurance company's assessments as "defence medicals" just to keep things clear.

It's not enough to just say someone can't work at their former job because their back hurts; **we must provide evidence showing the extent of your injuries.**

Before mediation, there's a good chance we'll ask you to attend an IME. Generally, we need them done after you've been to discovery but before mediation.

We typically do not get IMEs where the injuries are objective and well documented, such as when someone has a fracture, has had surgery, has an operative report, and/or has X-rays showing the fracture. However, sometimes even with objective injuries, we need an opinion about what the future holds for you and what care you'll need.

You may wonder why we don't just get your family doctor to answer our questions. Sometimes we will do this. However, family doctors are often very busy and they don't always have the time or experience to write the detailed type of report we need.

The IME doctor will start the process with your own medical records, past and current. These contain notes and records about your condition made by medical professionals and referring specialists. It's helpful information, but it tends to focus on injuries and treatment. Our goal is fill in the gaps. For example, the IME doctor will comment on how the accident caused the injuries. Your treating doctors don't care very much about the cause of your injuries. They just want to help you get better or manage your symptoms. The IME doctor will also consider what the injuries could mean for your future. Your treating doctors are probably not thinking about the long-term care for your problems except in the most catastrophic cases. The independent experts we hire to do additional exams depend on the kind of problem; for example, for spinal nerve damage, we may ask a neurosurgeon, while for soft-tissue injuries, a physiatrist.

Ahead of the assessment, we send the expert your medical records and a letter with eight to ten questions written specifically for your case. The question samples below are ones we believe are going to support your case when they are answered.

- **Diagnosis:** Is it your opinion that the diagnosis is the result of the motor vehicle accident? If so, please explain how the accident would have caused the injuries.

- **Prognosis:** Do you expect the patient to get better over time or to deteriorate?

- **Income losses:** Is this person likely to have difficulty doing specific or repetitive movements such as crouching, kneeling, stooping, or bending? (This would be relevant if they are an electrician and need to access small places.)

- **Future care:** What care (e.g., long-term physiotherapy or psychological care) will the client require over a lifetime? Are there medications that may be contra-indicated?

CASE STUDY: A thorough IME anticipates future questions

A figure skater client of ours suffered injuries in an accident. Based on the injuries, we knew there was no way he would ever skate again. No information about his ability to skate, however, appeared in his medical records because it wasn't considered relevant to treatment.

We anticipated that, at some point during the case, the defence would likely ask, "Have any of your doctors ever told you that because of your injuries you won't be able to return to figure skating?"

We obtained an expert opinion through an IME to answer such questions with factual evidence.

Are these doctors going to believe me?

The idea of a medical assessment can be a bit daunting. Some doctor is going to be poking around to find out what hurts when you've likely been through months of treatment already.

Be assured: there are no nasty surprises with the IMEs we set up for our clients. The process isn't going to damage your case.

After we've sent the doctor your records, and the doctor has seen you, we ask them if they will be able to give us a supportive opinion. Sometimes the doctor does not think the injuries were caused by the accident. In those situations, we say thank you very much, pay them for their time, and do not request a report. That opinion stays between us.

There's more to picking experts than Googling them

We know that when a jury hears an opinion from an authority, they're likely to nod and say, "Okay," so we take measures to make sure that the opinion evidence we obtain through an IME is credible, relevant, and perceived as unbiased.

We're good at selecting the right experts (it helps a lot to have been in the business so many years), and we use experts known to do assessments for both sides (ours and the defence). This works in our favour—it has built us a reputation for IMEs that aren't perceived as biased. If your case goes to trial, our assessments stand up in court.

As for the defence medical exams...

The previous explanation of what to expect from the medical exams we organize *does not apply* to defence medicals! Here's why.

The goal of a defence medical is to make sure that your physical condition corresponds with the extent and symptoms of the injuries you described (so far, so good). However, defence medicals tend to be defence oriented. Unlike the experts we engage, the experts hired by the defence typically only do assessments for insurance companies. They are specifically trying to catch you being dishonest. That is a big part of what they do.

As a result, the various tests carried out during an assessment are generally intended to reveal that someone is malingering—that is, exaggerating their pain and suffering. Wow. That probably doesn't make you feel so great about attending a defence medical.

But don't worry—it's going to be okay. Here's why. Success depends on knowing the kinds of tests and techniques that likely are going to be part of examination and then following a few simple rules.

Let's look at the various tests first.

Tricks, tactics, and downright sneaky maneuvers to watch out for

Window tests before you enter the building

Assessment rooms are set up so that the doctor or someone in the office can observe you walking in from the parking lot. Hey, you looked fine until you entered the examination room. Now you are limping and talking about how much it hurts. The assessor writes in your report, "On assessment, movement was guarded but otherwise free flowing" (translation: she was putting on a show for me).

Observation tests while you're chatting

Let's say you are describing severe pain in your neck but while you're talking with the expert ahead of the exam, he points out the window and you fall for the trick—you turn and look. Now you've demonstrated that your neck isn't that bad after all. You've also shown that when you talk about pain, you are faking or at least exaggerating.

Mobility and movement tests during the exam

There are various physical tests for checking to see if someone is faking pain. Two common ones are Waddell's straight leg test and the axial loading test for lower back pain. During axial loading, for example, the doctor presses on top of the

We give the same advice for a defence medical that we give ahead of discovery and mediation: **just be honest.**

patient's head and asks if this increases lower back pain. The patient, thinking that they are supposed to say yes, says it does. But the doctor knows that such a test never causes lower back pain. Gotcha!

Video surveillance before you arrive

There's a possibility that without your knowledge, you are followed and videotaped ahead of (or after) your appointment. For instance, you could be videotaped when you stopped to buy groceries and loaded them into your car, or when you visited a restaurant for breakfast ahead of time and sat for over an hour happily enjoying your coffee. Now you show up at your appointment, limping and finding it difficult to get comfortable in a chair.

The doctor writes in the assessment, "The person I saw on this video was very different from the person who showed up walking slowly and talking about pain in my office." Needless to say, this kind of documentation is very bad for your case.

Written psychometric tests during or afterwards

The exam may include a cognitive ability test. Don't try to force a result. These come with built-in validity questions scientifically designed so that certain answers reveal if you are trying to make something sound worse than it is.

Just be honest

In addition to assessing your physical condition, the expert carrying out a defence medical is trying to assess your nature, to determine if you're credible and sincere. They may, for instance, ask similar questions over and over again to see if you can be tricked into contradicting an earlier claim. There's a difference between severe pain that means you cannot stand for more than a few minutes and discomfort that doesn't seem to be an issue when you are out shopping.

We give the same advice for a defence medical that we give ahead of discovery and mediation: just be honest. It is really, really important that you don't report pain where it doesn't exist and don't describe the pain or the conditions it has caused as worse than they are. This can be a temptation even for the most honest people. Somehow, it just seems like the right thing to exaggerate a bit. You might even think it is going to help us out if you talk a lot about pain.

Don't do it.

If the doctor asks you to move a certain way and you don't experience any pain, then tell them so. If it hurts a lot, tell them that, using words like the ones we talked about in how to describe pain in Chapter 8 on discovery.

Bottom line: be truthful. There are too many pitfalls. You're not going to outsmart these doctors, especially if they have a videotape showing you moving more easily under different circumstances.

Defence medicals can actually help

A bad defence medical can make it difficult to settle your case at mediation. But if the defence assessor supports your case, it really helps a lot. This is especially true for people who are seriously injured.

A few years ago, we had a case of a woman in her 30s who was rear-ended on the highway. She was sent to a defence medical exam that confirmed the extent of her injuries. She received a settlement of $300,000 following a pre-trial conference.

What if I get a bad report?

If your defence medical comes back and it totally rejects our claims, or its contents don't align with your memory of what happened at the assessment, all is not lost. In fact, this happens more than 50 percent of the time. This is another instance where we advocate on your behalf.

Our experts are more expert than their experts

Once we have reports in hand from both sides, we can send the defence report to our own expert to get a follow-up opinion. This can be very helpful when our own expert has more experience or is known for their reputation in an area of medicine specific to your injury.

We won't let you be defeated by defence medicals based on outdated science

Medical understanding for conditions such as chronic pain, fibromyalgia, and concussions have greatly advanced over the past 15 years. But we still hear a doctor say things like, "There's no objective evidence for chronic pain" (myth busted) or the "normal" time for concussion recovery is three to six months (another myth busted—thank you, Sidney Crosby).

By depending on our experts to educate us, and keeping up-to-date with the latest medicine, we know how to debunk myths and rely on current, proven, and evidence-based findings.

Will the defence medical stand up in court?

There are other ways that our firm can investigate defence assessments to see how well they might stand up in court. Perhaps there were mistakes made, something was overlooked, or the expert wasn't qualified to comment on a certain area.

Then there is biased opinion—something that has given some defence-orientated experts the unfortunate title of a "hired gun." Biased opinion can make a defence's case vulnerable if it goes to trial; under cross-examination, we, as your lawyers, can point this out.

CASE STUDY: We've taken on "experts" in court and would do it again

A few years ago in court, our firm challenged a decision based on the expert testimony of a well-known psychiatrist. The expert had persuaded the jury that our client—a seriously injured woman—was "faking it," even though we had evidence that the crash had left her with chronic pain, depression, PTSD, and other troubles, which made a return to work untenable. The jury agreed that there was liability, but the damages they awarded were so low that they didn't even pass the deductible. However, we knew that this particular expert was known for his biased medical evidence. While the jury was deliberating, the defence called for a "threshold motion." This meant the judge had to rule on the question of "whether or not there was a serious and permanent injury of an important function."

Brenda had cross-examined the psychiatrist during the trial itself, confident that the quality of evidence our firm had gathered would reveal the bias and incompetence of this so-called expert. The judge agreed, ruling yes on the threshold decision. In his decision on the threshold, the judge chastened the psychiatrist for biased, invented evidence in the guise of being a medical expert. Ultimately, on an appeal, it was determined that allowing such a defence expert to testify was a "miscarriage of justice" and the only remedy was to order a new trial.

The judge's decision has since been called a game-changer for personal injury claimants, an indication that the courts have "had enough of the manipulations of insurers to delay and deny claimants through the use of biased medical evidence." The other good news? The "expert" psychiatrist has never done medical assessment since.

Independent medical exams: what you need to know

WHEN? Our IMEs are held after discovery and before mediation. If your case goes to trial, we may send you back for an updated assessment so your file is fresh. Most defence medicals are not requested until a case gets closer to an actual trial.

WHERE? Experts tend to be located in large centres, such as Toronto. If this is the case, we'll send you where you need to go or bring the expert to you. The same applies to defence medicals—and they cover the expenses.

Bonus: we give you a copy of your assessment, which contains advice and referral suggestions. Now you have a report you can take to your family doctor and ask, "Can you help me implement these treatment recommendations?"

WHAT TO BRING? Ahead of your assessments, whether for us or the defence, we send a package of information for you to review ahead of time. It's wise to bring the following to your assessment:

- A list of current medications: drug names, dosage, frequency, and purpose

- A list of current therapies, with names of providers and frequency of attendance

- Prepared notes (or have it fresh in your head) of your past medical history

Again, be forthcoming. Assessors have your medical records. It hurts your case if you pretend something isn't there.

11

Pre-trial Conference: Another Kick at the Can

PERSONAL INJURY cases often settle at mediation or shortly afterwards—at least, that's what we've been telling you. But let's say your case hasn't settled, which is beginning to get you down. You don't want your "day in court." You just want it all behind you. So when there is talk of something called a pre-trial, you might be ready to yell out loud, "Will this ever end? Why can't they just get on with it?"

A pre-trial (short for pre-trial conference) certainly sounds like another arduous step in the process, but at this point in a lawsuit, it's a very good thing (and not very arduous on your part).

A pre-trial gives us another chance to settle your case fairly, or if we can't settle on everything, at least narrow the issues to be resolved so we *can* get on with it. This time, instead of a mediator, we're going to meet with an authoritative figure—an actual, real-life judge—who is going to review the facts and issues and use their years of experience in these matters (and totally objective position) to give an opinion on the strengths and weaknesses of each party's case.

All of this means that there is everything to be gained from pre-trial and nothing to be lost.

Purpose of a pre-trial

Pre-trial conferences used to be called "settlement confer-ences." It's good to still think of them this way. There's a judge and there's a courtroom, but unlike at an actual trial, the pur-pose is not to decide the matter, and no one "takes the stand." The purpose is two-fold:

1 **Management:** The management part deals with functional issues related to getting ready for a trial, such as fixing the date and length, setting out a timetable for exchanging documents, looking at any special requirements or unusual motions, and so on.

2 **Settlement:** The settlement part is another opportunity to promote settlement, or at least narrow the contentious issues to be negotiated under one or both of the following areas: who was responsible for the collision (liability) and what the injuries are worth (damages). These are real, prac-tical matters that a judge alone can address at this point by simplifying, shortening, or narrowing the issues.

Take, for example, a car accident where someone was hit from behind. There is no question as to fault under Ontario law when it comes to rear-end collisions (the driver who hit the other is always at fault). So at a pre-trial, the judge may press the two sides to get rid of the liability issue and instead focus on the damages—that is, what the injuries are worth in dollars and cents.

Setting a pre-trial date

Pre-trial is booked once mediation has failed (or if there hasn't been any mediation). As your lawyers, we file the trial record, which is a copy of all the pleadings (the formal documents that exist on the file) and ask for a date to be set.

Patience, again. It could be a year from the time we make the request to when the pre-trial happens, particularly given the backlog of cases in Ontario. If this happens, we may send you for an updated medical assessment, and we then update your medical report and records such as additional financial losses and out-of-pocket expenses.

You've guessed it—it's time for another brief: a pre-trial brief. This brief sets out our position but contains nothing about any previous settlement offers. Our brief is delivered to the pre-trial judge, with a copy sent to the other side.

Courts require that the brief be no longer than ten pages, so what we prepare is less detailed than the mediation brief. This can be quite disappointing to clients who were wowed by our presentation at mediation. But those are the rules. As a result, we spend a lot of time preparing your pre-trial brief so it is still very effective in telling your story in the format required by the court.

A judge presides over the pre-trial. We don't get to pick who it is, but we are told their name ahead of time. (It helps that we know everyone.) Your prep ahead of the day will be a heads-up on what to expect from this particular judge, and we'll talk again about settlement numbers.

What happens? It depends on the judge

No two pre-trials are the same. Each judge handles the time in their own way. Often both sides are asked to present, but there are many times when the judge does most of the talking. They will talk about what they understand about the case after reading both briefs. There are opportunities for us lawyers to add another angle to what was said, if relevant, but in general it's up to the judge whether or not they want to hear from us. Once the plenary session (the management part we just described) is over, both sides break off into separate rooms and then offers are shuttled back and forth.

Will the judge address me?

You probably won't be asked to talk during the plenary session. Be warned, however, that some judges like to ask you questions directly, almost like during a cross-examination. They are "testing the water," similar to what you experienced at discovery. They want to assess how you'll come across in court—not to make you uncomfortable but to look for factors to support an eventual recommendation about issues either side could face at trial.

There is nothing you need to be braced for ahead of a pre-trial: no one feels shamed or humiliated, and there's no transcript that records everything you've said. There are more formalities than in a mediation; you'll hear terms like "Your Honour" and observe other rules of decorum, but the experience will feel much like mediation.

If we settle, great; if not, later that day or the next, we'll make time to talk about what happened and next steps.

Who are these judges?

Ideally, the judge assigned to a pre-trial for a personal injury case has experience in this area of the law. In any case, be

We want to hear what that judge has to say! **It's gold.**

assured that judges are highly respected, experienced, and knowledgeable in the law. They likely have presided over hundreds of cases, dealt with lawyers of all stripes, and have years of experience in understanding how cases like yours are dealt with at trial.

All of this means that they are very good at spotting weaknesses in a case, and knowing where the risks are, if a case goes to trial. Their role is to take a practical approach, based on their perspective on how the facts would be accepted. At pre-trial, they usually share this information in terms of an "opinion"— and we're glad that they do.

This is usually the most valuable part of a pre-trial, for both sides. It is *very* different from an actual trial where the judge and sometimes jury make a decision. By pointing out the strengths and weaknesses on each side, we all now have a much better idea of the risk factors in going to trial, and what issues we should focus on—and what to let go.

There are times when even good lawyers need a reality check. Let's say both sides have dug in their heels and negotiations on all fronts have come to a standstill. A pre-trial judge might grab the lawyers by the ears and force them to narrow the issues or do a reality check on what they are asking for— perhaps, throw them both outside and say, "Come back to me when you are reasonable with your estimate." (Just to be clear, this is not literal. No one will be tossed at a pre-trial.)

Do we really want the judge's opinion? Yes!

We most certainly do. As we prepare your case, we imagine how a fictional judge would see, hear, and interpret our side of the story. Our imagination is based on our extensive experience but it's still imagination. Now we have a real, live judge who has sat on many cases like yours and who has seen how juries react to cases like yours—over and over. Yes, we want to hear what that judge has to say! It's gold.

Could we hear about cracks in our case? Yes, we could. Some cracks we may know about and be trying to downplay. Some may take us by surprise. Either way, it's better to hear it in a pre-trial, when we have a chance to fix it, than to hear it for the first time at the end of a trial with a disappointing result.

The cracks work both ways. Through the judge's opinion, we also learn about the other side's case: the nuances and theories that make it weak, and the places we can probe that we otherwise wouldn't have known about.

Judges have additional "superpowers"

A pre-trial judge has a lot of power to make orders if someone is being a nuisance. For instance, maybe the other side has been dragging their feet to respond to a specialist expert report that we've submitted, or they keep coming up with "scheduling problems." A judge can—and will—step in and tell them to knock it off.

CASE STUDY: Is this argument likely to be successful at trial?

One of the most difficult kind of losses to prove are those connected to income from a new business venture. Unfortunately, we see this a lot. The accident victim is an entrepreneur about to start a new business just before she is seriously injured in an accident. She'd been very optimistic about the business idea, with plans in place and expectations for the new company to

If we do not agree with the judge's assessment—which does happen—**we are free to take it or leave it, as long as we do so respectfully and thoughtfully.**

take off. Initial sales were estimated at $100,000, and she believed it would provide a steady income until she turned 65. Then the business would be sold for a big profit.

This is where a judge takes on the role of managing expectations as to what kind of settlement is even possible. They know from experience how difficult it could be to prove the above argument at trial. After reviewing what kind of certainty existed to prove that such income projections were credible, they can give an opinion on whether the loss of income claim is likely to be successful.

Sometimes they are even more helpful and tell you that they think you have a 40 to 60 percent likelihood of success on that argument, which helps you understand how firmly you should stick to your settlement numbers.

What if we don't like what the judge says?
....

Hearing from a judge that you have a difficult case is never easy to swallow. But we're up for it and welcome this input, because the goal is always to get you as much money as soon as possible, without risk. If we do not agree with the judge's assessment—which does happen—we are free to take it or leave it, as long as we do so respectfully and thought-fully. Either way, the process gives us more information to help us continue to build your case in order to get you that settlement—and that's what we're going to do.

We also believe that we have a professional obligation to make sure that you understand what the judge's opinion means in terms of risk. You don't want a law firm that keeps certain aspects of a case hidden from their clients. That's not how we run our practice. Together, we review the strengths and weaknesses pointed out by the judge, and the risks we could face at a trial. We know how to work with what we've found out, and we know what a fair settlement should look like. We've done this hundreds of times, and we're good at it.

Booking a trial
....

If a settlement is not reached, the judge completes a "trial scheduling endorsement form" to indicate that the case did not settle. There's a synopsis of the case and a list of witness statements attached to the file. The judge then predicts the length of the trial and sets out a timetable for what has to hap-pen before that date.

The judge destroys their notes so that nothing about their opinion or the settlement amounts discussed goes into the record. (Remember, there is no transcript, and everything said at pre-trial is off the record.)

All is not lost if we haven't settled at pre-trial

Often, after hearing a judge's opinion about a matter, parties tend to become less entrenched in their positions. In fact, just having a fixed trial date motivates the parties to continue to work toward a settlement. It also provides a deadline for the resolution of the case—the trial date.

There's also the chance that the court will invite you to another pre-trial in order to put on another squeeze to settle.

CASE STUDY: Good things can happen at pre-trial

Stan's car was struck by a delivery truck and he suffered serious injuries. Despite his seatbelt, Stan's body whipped forward and back during the impacts, and Stan struck his head on the headrest.

Our lawyers helped to prepare Stan for the lawsuit against the driver who hit him and the company that owned the delivery truck. The examination for discovery was a success. Stan and his wife, Linda, were able to describe how the accident had impacted his life and what they had lost. The at-fault driver admitted that he was following too closely and did not allow himself time to brake.

Given the success at the examination, we had high hopes for mediation. However, the insurance company came to mediation unprepared. They offered a low six-figure amount that would not nearly be enough to compensate Stan for his losses. Stan was nervous about refusing the offer, but our team reassured him that his case was worth significantly more.

Determined to help Stan reach a fair settlement, our team continued to build Stan's case. We spoke to his employer and colleagues to gather additional evidence in support of his substantial loss of future income claim. We asked the court for a pre-trial date and attended a pre-trial with a judge, the insurance company's representative and lawyer, and, of course, Stan and Linda.

At the pre-trial, we helped Stan reach a settlement offer that was nine times more than we had been offered at mediation. Stan and Linda accepted.

Pre-trial: what you need to know

WHO? A judge, plus you and your lawyer. The lawyer for the defence (usually hired by the insurance company) and a representative of the defence, usually a claims examiner or adjuster, will also be present. If there is more than one client, they all must be available, at least by phone.

WHERE? This time, at an actual courthouse, perhaps in a courtroom or a small boardroom. Or virtually.

HOW LONG? Two hours, half a day, a day—it's our choice.

WHAT'S THE DRESS CODE? You guessed it. Professional, grown-up, like you dressed for discovery and mediation.

12

Going to Trial: We Can, We Will, and We Do

AFTER ALL these months trying to negotiate a fair settlement, now we tell you that a date has been set for a trial. Are we willing—and prepared—to go to trial? If the other side leaves us with no choice by failing to make a decent offer, you bet. We will always happily take your case to trial if that's what is needed to get fair compensation.

There are times when the insurance company digs in and the gap is too far to bridge. We've built a case that proves damages and losses at $250,000, but the defence insists that the pain and suffering still keeping you up at night is the result of medical issues you had before you were hit by a truck. They've assessed the risk of going to trial, and either believe that it is worth the risk or that we will cave at the last minute and accept an unsatisfactory award.

Hang in there. It's not over until it's over— and we're good at the "over" part

You may be feeling pretty frustrated that it's come to this, especially if it was clear that you were not at fault and your life has been changed by medical conditions caused by your injuries. Clearly not everyone believes you (the insurance people, that is). This reality can hit hard.

The decision to keep proceeding, of course, is yours. But keep this in mind: it is *still* very likely that your case will settle—ahead of the trial or even in the middle of the trial!

We are a firm that will go to trial, and this is where we add real value—the insurance companies and their defence lawyers know this, and they know we come to each case well prepared. Richard, for example, is our not-so-secret weapon. He brings years of experience in both criminal and civil law, with experience in more than 100 trials—an achievement many personal injury lawyers can't claim. This kind of trial experience can be a real game-changer.

Know that we are going to advise you on what we believe is in your best interest. We'll guide you through this final stage while we get your case ready for trial, and take on the months of preparation required to gather all the documents, arrange for witnesses, and prepare medical opinions. This is the culmination of all we've been doing since you first came to see us: building your case and taking it through discovery, mediation, medical exams, and pre-trial.

Preparation fit for D-day

Starting six to eight months ahead of the trial date, our firm switches into trial mode. Working back from the date, we develop long and detailed checklists with dozens of to-dos: notifying the expert witness and the lay witnesses, sending summons to witnesses, researching specific issues we think are going to come up, ordering exhibits such as photos and maps, and on and on.

As the trial date approaches (two months out), our trial team focuses on the witnesses. We'll outline all of the examinations for each witness—that is, what we are going to ask our own witnesses, and what we are going to cover when we cross-examine the witnesses called by the other side. There are meetings scheduled with witnesses, including perhaps visits to the family doctor or expert opinion witnesses.

Remember the kid in school who always studied for an exam at the last minute? That's not us. We don't do things by the seat of our pants—and it pays off, and not just in our results. It also builds our reputation; the insurance companies see us coming and know we are serious.

Every step of the way we are sending the message: "Do you really want to take this risk with a firm that's so on top of things?"

In the courtroom

Many personal injury trials in Ontario are conducted in front of a six-person jury. Cases against municipalities are a significant exception—these are almost never done with a jury. Cases with a dollar value below $200,000 are also exempt from juries.

For jury cases, the first day in court starts with jury selection. The panel is selected fairly quickly. If you've watched TV-show trials with science experts like "Dr. Bull," you're going to be disappointed. There are no questions about attitude, opinions, or preconceived ideas in Ontario. The only questions we can ask are related to their names, addresses, and employment. We do recommend that you be there with us because it's important that no one is selected that you know or even recognize.

Do I have to attend the trial?

We usually advise that you not sit through the entire trial, even though you are allowed to. If you do, the jury will no doubt spend a lot of time looking at you and thinking, "Hmmm, if she can sit here every day, maybe she could work?" "Is he rubbing his neck on purpose?" "Does she really need that ObusForme cushion, or is she using it as a prop?"

Some of the testimony may also be difficult to hear, especially if friends or relatives are asked about changes in your personality or demeanour. You don't want our witnesses to be less than frank to avoid hurting your feelings.

The next step—often on the same day following jury selection—typically involves procedural things that the lawyers work out with the judge related to the trial process. For example, there are a number of preliminary issues that the judge needs to assist with and which require rulings, such as the inclusion of particular evidence and pre-trial motions.

Okay, now we get to the courtroom action. It's not what you might imagine. There's likely no one watching in the gallery, except maybe some students. You are likely sitting on your own at the back, and most of the time we're going to advise that you not be there at all.

As your lawyer, we make our opening statement first. The insurance defence lawyer may follow or choose to wait until mid-trial. We are not allowed to be over the top in our opening statements. You might wish we were more like we were at mediation. Unfortunately, there are rules that keep the openings pretty cut and dried. Once the opening statements are complete, we start presenting your evidence.

Evidence takes the form of a witness answering questions or through the presentation of documents, such as the transcript of the defendant taken at discovery. Generally, the first witness is you—the plaintiff—followed by your spouse/partner. There are usually a few lay witnesses plus your family doctor who provided treatment, the attending police officer, one or two expert witnesses for medical issues, and perhaps an accounting expert and an expert witness qualified to speak to the issues of liability for the injuries. We ask questions, and then our witnesses are cross-examined by the defence. After all our witnesses have been examined by us and cross-examined by the defence, and all our exhibits have been entered into evidence, our case is considered closed.

Demonstrating the story

With all the documentation and witness evidence, it can be a challenge to see how everything in a case fits together. The judge, and in particular the jury, are dealing with medical jargon and details, like "How is an injury in one side of the body affecting movement in another? And what was the name of that condition again?"

This is why we try to make as much of our presentation as we can demonstrative. A lot of thought is put into pulling together photographs that demonstrate what happened, videos of before and after the accident, medical illustrations that show the injuries in a diagram, and even playing recorded telephone calls.

The lawyer for the insurance company is next. As the defence, they call their own witnesses and enter documents into evidence in order to establish their version of your case. We do the cross-examination this time. When the insurance defence lawyer has finished, we also have the opportunity to present reply evidence. "Reply evidence" is evidence that has come up during the cross-examination (not ahead of time) that we want to ask about or elaborate on.

Once all the evidence is presented and the cross-examinations are done, both lawyers present closing statements. Given that the medical evidence is likely to be complicated in cases that end up at trial, we see our closing statements as a final chance to help the jurors, and the judge, figure out how everything fits together and to understand without a doubt that your claim is fair and reasonable.

The judge then charges the jury with an address to make sure they understand the legal context of the issues they need to determine and how they are to make their decision. Sit back and relax. Sometimes this address is hundreds of pages long.

In a personal injury trial, the jury is also asked to answer a list of questions. These are very specific and are designed so the jurors provide reasons for their verdict. (See the list on page 192.)

Unlike in a criminal trial, jurors in a personal injury trial are not sequestered—holed up in a hotel room somewhere without access to media or the internet. For this reason, we suggest you make sure all your social media is private during the trial. Otherwise, you can be sure that someone will be checking your Facebook page, even if they are told not to. You don't want that!

It's unusual for a jury to take more than a couple of days to decide. Often it is just hours. Once the jury arrives at a verdict, the parties are contacted and assembled in the courtroom. The jury is then brought in and asked if they have arrived at a verdict. Once the judge has ensured that all jurors have arrived at a free and unbiased decision, the jury's answers are read.

Be truthful, accurate, and authentic.

If the trial has been conducted before a judge, it could be a few days or weeks before a verdict is reached.

Flaws in the system

In a motor vehicle case, damages for pain and suffering are reduced basically "behind the jury's back" by whatever the deductible is in the given year—approximately $40,000 unless the case is very serious. (This reduction does not happen in non-motor vehicle cases.) In other words, a jury could decide that you should get $100,000 for your pain and suffering and write that on their verdict answer sheet. The jurors will never know that you will only get $60,000 of that $100,000. The insurance company keeps the $40,000 for themselves.

Damages also get reduced in motor vehicle accidents by any amount that you receive from another source, such as long-term disability or extended health care benefits or accident benefits. The jury *does not get told this*, so in many instances, the jury members deduct it in their minds, figuring that this will avoid a double recovery amount. In reality, however, it results in a double deduction!

The jury's questions

Here are some draft questions for jurors to answer as they deliberate on a motor vehicle case. The questions would be similar for other personal injury cases.

1   Did the defendant's conduct in this case cause or contribute toward the plaintiff's injuries? (If you find that "but for"

the defendant's conduct the plaintiff would not have been injured, you must find the defendant caused the damages and is liable for them.) Yes _____ No _____

Regardless and independent of how you answered question 1, you must assess the amount of damages in each of the following questions.

2 General Damages to the Plaintiff (pain, injury, suffering, loss of enjoyment of life, past and future) $ _____

3 Loss of Care, Guidance, and Companionship to the Plaintiff's husband $ _____

4 Loss of Care, Guidance, and Companionship to the Plaintiff's son $ _____

5 Loss of Care, Guidance, and Companionship to the Plaintiff's daughter $ _____

6 Past Loss of Income (from the date of the accident to present) $ _____

7 Future Loss of Income

   a Are you satisfied on the evidence that there is a real and substantial possibility that the plaintiff will incur a loss of future income? Yes _____ No _____

   b If your answer to 7 (a) is yes, what do you calculate the loss to be? $ _____

   c By what percentage if any should the calculation in para. 7 (b) be reduced to reflect additional contingencies? _____%

8   Future Care Costs

    a   Are you satisfied on the evidence that there is a real and substantial possibility that the plaintiff will incur future care costs? Yes _____ No _____

    b   If your answer to 8 (a) is yes, what do you calculate the loss to be? $ _____

    c   By what percentage if any should the calculation in para. 8 (b) be reduced to reflect additional contingencies? _____%

9   Future Home Maintenance

    a   Are you satisfied on the evidence that there is a real and substantial possibility that the plaintiff will incur future home maintenance costs? Yes _____ No _____

    b   If your answer to 9 (a) is yes, what do you calculate the loss to be? $ _____

    c   By what percentage if any should the calculation in para. 9 (b) be reduced to reflect additional contingencies? _____%

10   Special Damages $ _____

Prepping for your day in court

We hold between three to five meetings with you ahead of a trial to help you prepare your testimony and practice being cross-examined. We also prepare partners/spouses. Our playbook is the transcript taken at discovery. We have you read it, so we can make sure that when you are asked the same questions at trial, you don't contradict yourself.

Being impeached has nothing to do with being president

Being "impeached" at trial means that your testimony is discredited because the other side can prove with contrary evidence that you have not told the truth or your testimony has been inconsistent.

Various tools can help you feel more comfortable with what's going to happen when you are actually on the stand. For instance, we film you so you can review how you answer questions and check your body language. When you talk about what happened, does your story resonate with others? We often use a six-person focus group of non-lawyers to do a mock trial so that we can get feedback on the kinds of issues that may come up and give you a sense of what the trial experience will be like.

Our goal is to make sure that you present yourself in the best possible light when you testify. Nothing fake. For instance, we're not asking for a shiny new suit if that's not what you wear—ever. It would only make you come across as uncomfortable. Don't make this the day to decide to wear an outlandish wig or dress entirely in leather. Part of coming across well is showing up without any chip on your shoulder or "principle to prove."

We're not exaggerating here. We once had a client who showed up in a hoodie bearing the image of a machine gun! (He missed the memo.)

The general advice we give is simple: don't exaggerate. Don't try to be cute. Don't make jokes. You're not going to

There is no trial by ambush in a personal injury trial. The principles of mutual disclosure apply.

fool anybody. You're not going to trick the other lawyer or the judge. It's what we've said from day one, and at this point, it may sound trite: be truthful, accurate, and authentic.

The dreaded cross-examination

You've seen it in TV shows: at the last minute, some terrible secret is revealed and everyone in the courtroom gasps. This isn't going to happen. There is no trial by ambush in a personal injury trial. The principles of mutual disclosure apply. This means that, as your lawyers, we have to share with the defence in advance everything we are going to tender as evidence, and the insurance defence lawyers have to do the same.

There is one exception: video surveillance. The defence must disclose the fact that they have video, but they don't have to show it to us unless you make a direct contradiction on the stand. For instance, if you are asked if you're able to lift over two kilos and you say no, but the defence has a tape that shows you carrying your great Bernese mountain dog into your house—the tape can now be shown.

When cross-examining, lawyers have to walk a fine line to extract evidence that supports their case strategically and in a way that isn't abusive. Part of a judge's role is to make sure you are treated respectfully. They won't tolerate hostile, aggressive cross-examination. This doesn't mean that you won't be confronted with some difficult questions. But if you are cross-examined on some small detail that happened five years ago, it isn't a memory test. If you can't remember, say so. (Just don't make something up!)

The "yes, yes, yes" routine

There are various cross-examination styles. One that we prepare you for is a series of rapid questions that seem to lead to an obvious "yes" answer. "Is it true that this happened?" Yes. "Is it true that you did this?" Yes. "Is it also true that you didn't do this?" Yes...

It's an effective way for the insurance defence to control the conversation by guiding you toward the answers their side wants. Part of our prep work is to help you recognize when this is happening and know that it's okay to pause and not get pulled in by the momentum.

Expect the unexpected

The steps leading to trial are routine. What comes up at a trial, however, can be very unpredictable. That's why after all these chapters, we keep saying that if we can avoid a trial and still get fair compensation, we will. But understanding what can happen at a trial is going to make you a better witness. It's also going to shed some more light on why the skills of your lawyer matter so much.

We know, within certain parameters, what we expect to hear because we've got the transcript from discovery, and we have the evidence and the witness statements from both sides. But a trial is an organic, fluid, human process. It's impossible to anticipate everything that could happen. Your lawyer has to be grounded, flexible, and unflappable.

Perhaps we thought that one of our witnesses was going to talk about something, but they didn't. We can't put words in anyone's mouth. Now we need to arrange for another witness to introduce that evidence. Or we thought that we'd prepared someone on how to answer a certain question, but they said something completely unexpected. This will happen in every single trial. The unpredictability of the trial is exciting, but it does create risk.

Success partly comes down to a trial lawyer knowing when and how to pivot in response to the day's evidence. This continues right up to when we write our closing statements, adjusting what we say to reflect what's happened over the course of the trial, so we can help the jury understand that your claim is fair and reasonable.

What if things go wrong?
....

Given that more than 90 percent of personal injury cases settle without a trial, if your case is one that goes to trial, it may have some special challenges. Maybe there is a debate about who caused the accident. Maybe it is unclear if your medical issues were caused by the accident or something else, such as a pre-existing condition. If your case goes to trial, be assured that we will do everything in our power to achieve the best possible result. Having said that, there is no guarantee of success.

So what happens if the case is unsuccessful at trial? In some situations, it is possible to appeal an unsuccessful personal injury verdict. An appeal is a process that allows us to ask a higher court to overturn the trial judge's or jury's decision. To appeal, we usually must find some serious error that affected the outcome of the case. Advancing an appeal can be a costly, high-risk proposition, but where a mistake was made at trial, it can be your best bet for securing a just outcome. A full step-by-step analysis of the appeal process is outside the scope of this book, but it is important to know that the right of appeal exists.

Some clients wonder if they could owe money to someone after an unsuccessful trial. The short answer is a lawyerly one: maybe yes, maybe no. In Ontario, the normal rule is that the unsuccessful party must pay some of the legal fees of the successful party. Those costs can be significant, running into the six figures. If you purchased cost insurance, you would have an amount available to cover the defendant's legal fees if the court awards costs against you. Many of our clients have purchased affordable costs-protection policies worth $100,000 or more to minimize this risk. (On the plus side, if we are successful at trial, the defendants will have to pay some of your legal fees in addition to the amount awarded at trial.) At the time of writing this book, after 17 years in business, not one of our clients has ever had to pay costs to the opposing side after a trial. It could absolutely happen, but it is rare and has not happened yet.

If you hired us based on a contingency fee agreement, you will not have to pay any legal fees to us if we are unsuccessful at trial. However, we may have out-of-pocket expenses known as disbursements that you would pay for. If you have purchased cost insurance, a portion of that insurance may cover these expenses as well.

If you are concerned about what could happen after an unsuccessful trial, speak to us. We'll explain the specific risks of your case, so you can make an informed decision about the risks and the benefits.

There's no "principle of the thing"— only getting you a fair result

Less than 5 percent of personal injury cases in Ontario ever go to trial. But we've had dozens of cases go right up to trial, only to settle on the courtroom steps. Occasionally we have a client who wants to go to trial "for the principle of the thing." This is not a good reason to have a trial. We are talking about insurance companies paying out money—there is no other principle of the thing. There will be no acknowledgement of wrongdoing or an apology. It's about getting you a fair result, and the chances of doing so are much better if we can avoid a trial altogether.

But yes, we can go, and it's no secret that when push comes to shove, we will go. Some cases need a trial to achieve a fair result. When this is true, we will take all steps necessary to handle the trial for you and obtain the best possible result.

Trial: what you need to know

WHEN? The trial date will be set at the pre-trial.

WHERE? A courtroom in the jurisdiction where you live, or virtually.

WHO ATTENDS? The plaintiff (you), the lawyers, a court reporter, witnesses, a judge, and a jury. You can also request a translator. We usually recommend that you not attend the entire trial.

HOW LONG? The length of the trial is set according to the complexity and number of witness. Could be five days or 12 weeks.

WHAT'S THE DRESS CODE? Be authentic. If you don't normally wear a suit, don't make yourself uncomfortable. Presentation matters, however: be well groomed and presentable, and avoid offensive slogans, high heels, baseball caps, and so on.

13

Settlement: When Does It Happen?

SOPHIE'S CASE looked like it would settle quickly. The 40-year-old was recovering well from her accident-related neck and back injuries. She was suffering from some knee pain when she came to see us, but so far no one had connected it to the accident. One doctor told her it was a sprain or strain, while another suggested it was a rare birth defect that was completely unrelated to the accident. With Sophie's agreement, we decided to wait, not settle, in order to get the appropriate diagnosis.

Fortunately, a third doctor finally took the time to perform more significant diagnostic testing on Sophie's knee. The result revealed a damaged meniscus resulting from the accident that required surgery. We settled this case for three times the amount we would have settled for if we had not waited.

Timing can be everything.

MANY CLIENTS have the impression that settlement happens when a case gets close to going to trial, and that all of this takes place within a year or so. Neither of these things are true. Settlement can occur at any point before or during litigation, and litigation can take months, even years. It's therefore not likely that a final result will be reached within a few months, except for quite small cases where we're able to avoid a lawsuit in the first place. Knowing at what point along the way to make this decision isn't something that can be taught—it's one of those instincts that experience teaches.

We start thinking about settlement on the first day we listen to your story. We ask ourselves, "Is this just going to take a phone call?" or "Is this a case that could go to trial?" or somewhere between. Then we turn our minds to considerations like, "What is it going to take to get this person fair compensation—and is it even going to be possible?"

It's always about you

Some clients worry that we will keep them at a distance when deciding on a settlement offer. They may wonder if they will even know that their lawyer is making an offer to settle.

You are not at the mercy of our decisions at Auger Hollingsworth. You are a participant in the process through us and in consultation with us. We'll have conversations along the way about the numbers and the settlement offer we propose *before* we propose it. You make the final decision.

Uncovering the unknowns

The big question on our minds is "What are the unknowns here?"

In every case, we are looking to answer these questions:

- What do we have and what do we need to prove liability?

- What do we have and what do we need to prove medical injury?

- What do we have and what do we need to prove financial losses?

We will counsel you not to settle your case **until you have reached maximum medical recovery.**

At first, there's just basic information to assess, such as the incident report or motor vehicle report, reports from the emergency room and your family doctor, and financial data, if there is evidence of a loss of income. In some cases, the unknowns solve themselves.

For instance, let's say that your injury was a straightforward ankle fracture. You fell in the supermarket because there was water on the floor from a leaky freezer. Liability and losses are clear. Medical records show that after a couple of months, the injury is healing well. Although you couldn't work for five months after the accident, you are now back at it and your job is going well.

This is an example where we have enough to answer all three of the key questions (liability, pain and suffering, financial losses), and there are no future unknowns. So at the earliest opportunity, we would propose a settlement.

Maximum medical recovery? Time will tell

One of our biggest concerns is that we might settle your case too early, before you know the full extent of your injuries. Once you have signed off on a settlement, there is no going back for more money if you learn about a new problem from the accident or your injuries turn out to be worse than you thought. For that reason, we will counsel you not to settle your case until you have reached maximum medical recovery.

The problem is, in most cases that are serious enough to pursue, it can take six to 18 months to get to maximum medical recovery. If you have had surgery for a broken ankle, for example, and you have pins and screws inserted, shouldn't you wait to see if you will have to have a second surgery to get the hardware out? Most of the time, hardware removal is easy and straightforward. What if yours isn't easy and straightforward? This is what keeps us up at night.

So if you are wondering why it is taking so long for us to even start settlement discussions, it may well be that the medical records, and your updates to us, are telling us your case isn't ready because your body isn't ready.

Why are we not offering to settle right now?

If we hold off on making a settlement offer, you know there's a reason (and we'll tell you what it is). It may be that we are waiting until we know what the future holds for you in terms of employment and your future care. If you are not yet back to work, or not working at full capacity, the insurance company is not going to pay full value for your loss of income until enough time has passed that it knows this situation is permanent.

After a serious motor vehicle accident where it is unknown whether you will qualify for catastrophic accident benefits, the insurance company for the at-fault driver is not going to pay full value for your future care costs until it knows whether or not these benefits will be covered by another insurance company. In many instances, we can't even apply for your catastrophic status until two years post-accident. This obviously affects not just the settlement amount but also when we would even propose a settlement.

Likewise, if there are criminal charges arising from the accident, we may have to wait until the criminal process has run its course before the police will release documents we need to prove liability for the accident. Rest assured, we are checking and pushing to get the documents, but personal injury cases are low on the police priority list, sadly.

A few years ago, we had a case where a three-year-old child was hit by a car and suffered catastrophic injuries. We were only able to settle when the boy turned ten, because by then we knew what the impact would be on his schooling and therefore his future earning potential. This is one of many cases where injuries are severe, and losses (medical and financial) are going to remain unknown for months, even years.

The time is right to settle when we are confident that we can assess the value of your case without too many unknowns. What we try to avoid is settling when some of your future is uncertain, such as your future employment prospects or your future medical needs.

Once you've signed the release for a settlement deal (see Chapter 14, page 221), you give up your future right to pursue the defendant. We want to make sure that everything is stable because you can't go back for more.

The time is right to settle when we are confident that **we can assess the value of your case without too many unknowns.**

How an insurance company looks at recovery

An insurance company is always going to assume that you are going to make the best possible recovery—that is its "known." So, if your recovery is going to be worse than what the insurance company might expect and it's hard to predict the outcome, we advise that, to get top dollar, we wait to show that you've plateaued in your recovery.

Opportunities for settlement

There are some stages in the lawsuit (even before it starts) where settlement is more likely to occur. You'll recognize these stages from previous chapters. Now you can see how they tie in with making a settlement proposal.

A negotiated settlement directly with the adjuster (no lawsuit!)

There are circumstances where we believe a case could settle by negotiating directly with the insurance adjuster (like the earlier example about the broken ankle). Liability isn't in doubt, and medical records, including updates, show that your injury level has remained constant over several months. Ideally, the adjuster feels the same way.

If you agree, we send a letter to see if the adjuster is willing to settle. Along with a settlement amount, we describe how the accident happened and why it was another person's fault. If there are aggravating factors we think would impact the value of the case, we describe them as well.

These types of early negotiations may go back and forth with offers and counteroffers over a few weeks. If a proposal is ultimately accepted, great. You've avoided the long process of a lawsuit and the risk of a trial. But if the response isn't favourable, we don't back down. Our job now is to start a lawsuit right away.

CASE STUDY

All kinds of cases can settle at the adjuster level. We represented a man in his 30s who had a bicycle accident because a driver opened his car door into traffic and our client flew over the door and landed on his shoulder. We settled with a direct negotiation with the adjuster and did not have to start a lawsuit. In another case, a man was killed as a pedestrian in a motor vehicle accident and his widow, son, and granddaughter received a substantial settlement through our negotiation with an insurance adjuster.

Settling before or just after a lawsuit (hey, they're serious!)

We see this a lot. We've tried to negotiate directly with the insurance adjuster. When that fails we issue a Statement of Claim to start a lawsuit. The adjuster receives a copy of the claim and takes another look at the case. He wakes up and says, "Oh, I get it, these people are serious." At that point, we may receive a better response to our previous settlement offer, or we may get an invitation to make an offer if we haven't already.

CASE STUDY

A few years ago, we represented an elderly gentleman who received a settlement following a rear-end collision on Preston Street in Ottawa. This man in his 80s received a healthy

six-figure settlement on account of the nerve damage he suffered in the accident. The case was resolved as soon as the
claim was filed.

In another case, a child was injured in the schoolyard when
a faulty fence bounced back at him and seriously cut his head.
We settled the case without a lawsuit.

Leading up to discovery (okay, let's talk)

Imagine the scenario that unfolds ahead of discovery. We've
sent all the records we've been gathering on your behalf since
you first hired us (in the exchange of documents). Without
bragging too much, it's a pretty impressive stack of evidence,
updates, and witness statements. The week before discovery,
the insurance company defence lawyer reviews what we've
sent and figures there's not much point going ahead with the
discovery since they have all the information they need to
assess the case.

CASE STUDY

A 54-year-old woman slipped in a grocery store aisle and fractured her kneecap, which required surgery to fix. Examination
for discovery was coming up quickly. We had met with our client and prepared her to testify. We were ready. However, as
the defence lawyer was prepping, she realized the case should
be settled. We got on the phone, and with our help, we settled our client's claim for $90,000 before examination for
discovery.

After discovery

The same situation happens after discovery (again, it's part
of our strategy: bury them in well-produced briefs and witness will-say statements). This time, you've played a role. The
defence has questioned you and sees how well you present

yourself as a straightforward, honest person who's been seriously injured. Next thing we know, we're invited to make a settlement offer.

CASE STUDY

We had a hardworking health care worker, a woman in her 30s, who did such a good job at discovery that the defence lawyer called and wanted to negotiate before mediation. She received $85,000, which was a great result for her specific injuries.

Mediation

This is when we get to tell your story in a compelling way that might even bring out emotion in an insurance adjuster. Not wanting a judge or jury to feel the same way, they may decide to settle then and there—a success. Once again, this is where a well-built case and presentation, with you there as a credible witness, gives the other side a sense of the risks they would be facing if the case went to trial. At this stage, we likely have conducted independent medical exams, so we have expert opinions on your losses.

Mediation discussions can take place during the day, at the end of the day, or in the days and weeks that follow. It's also not unusual for settlement discussions to start three to four months after mediation day.

CASE STUDY

A well-known restaurateur who fractured his hip slipping in an icy parking lot received $270,000 at mediation from the owner of the parking lot and the snow removal service.

In another case involving a hip injury, a woman in her 40s was rear-ended by a truck on her way to work. She suffered tears to both hips and one shoulder, and she suffered from chronic pain and psychological impairments. Her accident benefits insurer deemed her catastrophically impaired. Our firm helped her settle her tort (bodily injury) claim for $550,000 and her accident benefits claim for over $700,000, both at mediation.

Pre-trial conference

Your case looks like it may be heading for trial. A pre-trial conference provides another opportunity to settle. This can happen on the day of pre-trial, or any time right up until the trial starts (even the day before!).

CASE STUDY

We represented an industrious personal support worker who was having lunch at a fast-food restaurant when a piece of equipment fell on her leg. Her leg was so badly hurt that she couldn't put weight on it, which affected her life and her physical work. We settled her case at a pre-trial.

Where settlement approval is needed

Even when everyone has agreed on a settlement number, there's a final step if the injured person is a child or someone without capacity. In these cases, a judge must approve the settlement amount and the legal fees. It may seem like more waiting, but this supervisory role protects vulnerable people from negligence, unintentional errors, and outright fraud by unscrupulous lawyers.

As your lawyer, we have to personally make a sworn statement to explain why we think that a settlement is fair and include the evidence we've gathered to support the amount. We also have to explain the rationale behind our legal fees and the expenses we have incurred to fight the case. The litigation guardian, appointed to look after the best interests of the person under a disability, also has to swear an affidavit saying that they support the settlement.

Judges aren't going to accept some flimsy report for these kinds of serious settlements. And if they don't approve a settlement, it's a real mess.

We may be the lawyers, but you are always the decision-maker

You're suffering because of what you've been going through since your accident. Now the litigation itself feels like part of the suffering. So you ask us, "Can you just make a settlement proposal?"

We will give our opinion and advice, but you have the final say. If you tell us your goal is reaching a settlement without having to go to trial, we always listen to your input. You always make the final decision.

Masters of cool, calm, and steadfast negotiation skills

Our strategy is to be prepared to take a case to trial if a viable settlement is not reached. This is not an empty threat. The defence knows from our reputation that this is how we prepare each case. Adjusters see us coming and say, "Hey, these guys are for real—they'll take it all the way to trial if we don't get serious."

In addition, we have years of experience with negotiating, and we apply these skills when we enter into every settlement discussion:

- We're masters of the poker face. We know that if an adjuster ever sees or hears in our voice that we are satisfied with what amount is being suggested, we will never get higher than that amount.

- As described in Chapter 6, we always go into a negotiation with a target. This number cannot be pie-in-the-sky. It has to be something we can justify based on the evidence we have gathered, including expert opinions and the case law research we've done.

- There's a fine line between begging and looking desperate versus pursuing settlement vigorously. Our job is to walk that line.

- We are steadfast in our negotiation role. As long as the other side keeps sending back a number, we keep going. It sometimes means a dozen or more rounds.

- As you read earlier, both of us started out at large Bay Street law firms where we worked on the side of the defence. It was excellent training, but it opened our eyes. We both decided we wanted to help people who were injured or disabled because of an accident—not the insurance companies defending against you.

14

Closing the Case: Time for a Reset

THE LAWSUIT is finally over. It started with that first telephone call when you wondered if you even wanted to talk to a lawyer, let alone sue anyone. Now, you are going to receive a settlement cheque.

Depending on the type of case, there can be a variety of papers that need to be signed. There is often (but not always) some form of settlement agreement, often called Minutes of Settlement. There is always a Release that says that you cannot go back for more money once the deal is closed. For an accident benefit settlement, there is also a disclosure notice that the insurer has to provide.

We'll read the final terms of these documents with you line by line to make sure the information is accurate. Sometimes the insurance company adds something in about what you must agree to do, or perhaps a clause saying you promise not to talk about the amount or say bad things about what caused your slip and fall. These are obligations that should be negotiated, not just slipped in. If this is the case, we protect your interests—maybe insist they delete this, or up the compensation, or just say no.

Once these signed papers are received by the insurance company for the defence, a cheque is approved and sent to our office. We'll chase them down if it takes too long to get your cheque ready. It should take less than a month.

Managing a large settlement?

There are financial planners who specialize in maximizing settlement money from personal injury claims. This is not our speciality, but we can set up and host a meeting at our office before closing the final deal. No obligation, but it's a good idea to get some advice on how to structure a settlement in order to minimize tax implications and maximize your return.

For a settlement related to a child or a person who lacks capacity, as part of the court approval process you have to say what's going to happen to the money, so some advance financial planning will be required. We can help you with this.

The cheque is about the future, not the past

After all you have been through, receiving your cheque isn't going to feel that dramatic. No one releases balloons or white doves into the air. But we hear from clients over and over again that, in the end, it was worth it. There is always a sense of relief.

You hung in there through all the questioning, the meetings and phone calls, the doctors' appointments, and those uncomfortable times when you had to listen to the insurance defence lawyer talk about you—perhaps not in the nicest way. Now all of that is behind you. Finally, you can start trying things again, without fear that an insurance company is spying on you or checking to see whether or not you can do a certain type of job. You are finally free to just live your life, sign up for any treatments *you* want, see how much you can push yourself as you continue to rehabilitate, and make decisions without having to justify anything.

Think of that settlement cheque as **security for the future.**

For some, we hope that the money feels like some compensation for what you had to go through because of your accident. For those with catastrophic injuries, the money is more about security for the rest of your life. Going forward is not going to be easy, but we hope that at least you can now focus on living the best life you can, without the backdrop of financial worries.

The settlement cheque is never going to change what happened, and it's not going to change everything going forward. But think of that settlement cheque as security for the future. With the passage of time, and with continuing treatment and rehabilitation, most people do reach a new, if different, way of living. It's a reset that begins the process of getting your life back. Now, we hope that reset is possible.

Acknowledgements

WITHOUT THE thousands of clients who have put their faith in us over the past 17 years, this book would not have been possible. We are immensely grateful for your trust. All of the anecdotes and examples shared in this book are based on the lived experiences of resilient injured folks who continue to inspire us, even years later. The names and some identifying information have been changed but the stories are true. Special thanks (in no particular order) to Scott, Daniel, Kathy, Mohamad, Erin, Orlando, Rikki, Todd, Abdi, Guylaine, Jeremy, Kaitlyn, and Barb.

Resources

I F YOU are reading *The Road to Recovery* because you have been injured in an accident, you may be looking for some additional resources to help you manage your case. We have prepared some bonus materials to accompany this book for people going through their own accident case.

Remember, this is legal information and not legal advice and is intended for people who have been injured in Ontario.

Visit ahinjurylaw.com/the-road-to-recovery to access the following resources:

- How to give notice of a slip and fall claim to an Ontario municipality

- How to give notice after a slip and fall on ice or snow on private property in Ontario

- Questions to ask a lawyer at your initial client interview

- How law firms get paid using contingency fees

- The current monetary deductible that applies to an Ontario motor vehicle case

- The current cap on damages for pain and suffering and loss of enjoyment of life

- Documents that you should provide to the lawyer handling your accident case

- A guide to talking with your medical team after an accident

- How social media can wreck your accident case

- How a lawyer assesses the value of your personal injury case (video)

- How to prepare for examination for discovery (audio file)

- How to prepare for mediation (audio file)

- How to be a good witness at trial

We hope you find these resources helpful. Please reach out if Auger Hollingsworth Professional Corporation can assist you in any way.

About the Authors

RICHARD AUGER, B.A. (Hons.) LL.B., is an Ontario lawyer with a unique perspective, having practiced both criminal and civil litigation, and having represented both injured people and defendants. Richard has effectively handled more than 100 trials and has secured millions of dollars in settlements for his clients. He is known for his tireless preparation and fierce cross-examination, skills he has used to examine doctors, police officers, negligent drivers, property owners, and even a former prime minister. Richard is the managing partner at Auger Hollingsworth Professional Corporation, a firm he co-founded in 2005.

BRENDA HOLLINGSWORTH, M.A., LL.B., started her law career on Bay Street but knew very early that her calling was to help injured Ontarians get the compensation they deserve after suffering serious injuries. Brenda's personal commitment to her clients' well-being—financial, physical, and psychological—drives Auger Hollingsworth's approach to litigation and client service. Well-known in Ontario's personal injury bar, Brenda is frequently called upon to speak at educational events for other lawyers. A co-founder of Auger Hollingsworth, Brenda is the practice leader of the firm, responsible for designing, implementing, and supervising the firm's legal services. Under her leadership, the firm has garnered more than $105 million for its clients since its inception.

Richard and Brenda were called to the Ontario Bar in 1997. They are married to each other and have two grown sons.

CPSIA information can be obtained
at www.ICGtesting.com
Printed in the USA
JSHW010942230123
36518JS00004B/10